D1356121

# UTOPIA OR ELSE...

*Other works by the same author*

FALSE START IN AFRICA

IS CUBA SOCIALIST?

SOCIALISMS AND DEVELOPMENT
(with Marcel Mazoyer)

THE HUNGRY FUTURE
(with Bernard Rosier)

# René Dumont

# UTOPIA
# OR ELSE...

*Translated from the French by*
VIVIENNE MENKES

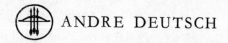 ANDRE DEUTSCH

First published 1974 by André Deutsch Limited
105 Great Russell Street London WC1

English translation © 1974 by André Deutsch Limited

Originally published in French under the title *L'Utopie ou la mort!*
© 1973 by Editions du Seuil

All rights reserved

Printed in Great Britain by
Lowe and Brydone (Printers) Ltd.
Thetford Norfolk

ISBN 233 96584 x

*To Suzanne Philippon, my companion;
to Béatrice, Catherine, Bernard and Claude*

# CONTENTS

# END OF A CIVILIZATION

Almost all my life I've felt thoroughly revolted by something. Even at the age of ten I was sickened by the frightful massacre of 1914, caused by the stupidity of our French generals and leaders from Joffre to Poincaré. Shortly after this Adolphe Gauthier, who had been the socialist member of parliament for Clamecy from 1910 to 1914, introduced me to socialism by making me aware of injustice. In 1917 some soldiers on leave told me all about those who had been 'executed as an example to others'. As early as 1923–4, when I was in Morocco and Tunisia, and particularly from 1929 to 1932 in the rice-fields tilled by the peasants of Vietnam – known in those days as 'Tonkinese' – I had a close-up view of the extreme poverty suffered by colonized peoples and of the disgrace of colonial oppression. Since I couldn't do anything about any of this – though I had at first thought I could – I returned to France.

The struggle against neo-colonialism is the logical sequel to the struggle that we were unable to wage against the 'French wars' in Indochina and Algeria from 1946 to 1962 because there were too few of us. For forty years now I've been trying, by means of studies in the field, discussions with colleagues, my classes at the 'Agro'* and in a good many other places, to make French people, other French-speaking nations and, later on, a broader spectrum of people (when my books began to be translated) aware of the fact that our capitalist economic system is totally unacceptable and that it

* The Institut National Agronomique in Paris (*translator's note*).

1

entails fundamental injustices, particularly on the global scale; and that this system of ours is that of a world that boasts of being free, deliberately forgetting that it is first and foremost the world of the rich.

Indeed I feel that the word 'unacceptable' has become pretty feeble now, particularly since the bombing of Vietnam in 1972 and especially the bombing of the dykes on the Red River, which were the result of a thousand years of un-remitting efforts. This feeling was reinforced when I read, in particular, Barbara Ward's and René Dubos's *Only One Earth*; the Club of Rome's *Limits to Growth*; *Blueprint for Survival* by the *Ecologist* group in London; Barry Commoner's *Closing Circle*; and Robert Lattés's *Pour une autre Croissance* etc.[1]

I felt as if someone had literally grabbed me by the throat when I took in the prospects forecast by books of this kind. They spoke of the total and inevitable collapse of our civiliza-tion at some point next century (a fair number of the French-women born in 1973 may well live through the first half of the twenty-first century, since their expectation of life is seventy-five) if the current exponential growth (with com-pound interest) in population and industrial output continues. But these books didn't entirely satisfy me – far from it.

I find it hard to understand why the Club of Rome, which was formed by the leaders of the capitalist economic system but also includes economists and scientists, fails to spell out more clearly the social and political consequences that can be deduced merely by examining their forecasts. The English naturalists who belong to the *Ecologist* group, who are after all scientists, should have been more outspoken in this respect. Whereas Ward and Dubos do plead the cause of the poor countries more successfully, none of the *Ecologist* authors names the people who are responsible for the terrible drama that is imminent. Yet we must name names. For the first time in history the best brains in the capitalist countries are admitting publicly that they're leading us to the brink of catastrophe – and that the catastrophe is imminent. It is therefore essential that we should look for a way out of the system – and quickly. According to M. Mazoyer (director of economic and social research at the 'Agro'), no human society has ever lost control of its population figures, its technology and its model of consumption on the same scale as we have.

The situation is made even worse by the fact that one of the most serious results of this type of research hasn't been sufficiently emphasized. By the time the 'underdeveloped' countries are eventually in a position to build up their own heavy industries from their own resources they will already have been robbed of most of their best minerals and oils. This will mean that they can never become even remotely competitive, and their expansion potential will be dreadfully restricted. It isn't just that we are heading for a violent breakdown of our type of civilization, to the detriment of our grandchildren. At the same time we are taking away for ever any hope, any real possibility for development from the countries with a dominated economic system, because of the increasingly unacceptable way in which we are squandering resources. W. W. Rostow told them that they must just wait patiently like good little children and they would definitely go through the same stages of development, though they would be a bit behind the others . . . . The fallacy inherent in his theses was demonstrated long ago (and indeed he even accused himself of promoting a false argument by advising Johnson in support of the war in Vietnam) – but now we've even got the capitalists denouncing it as fundamentally wrong-headed.

In Part I I dispose first of Herman Kahn's semi-lunatic forecasts, then I move on to list the main threats – soil degradation, malnutrition, the depletion of mineral reserves, overpopulation in the rich countries, air and water pollution, the danger of damage to the ecosystems and to climates and so on. Even if the data collected are still open to question, these threats make it impossible in the medium term for us to accept both the population explosion – particularly among the rich nations, who squander and pollute on a bigger scale – and an endless stepping up of industrial production, particularly in the field of arms, which represent an appalling danger. These threats are going to make the poor countries poorer, while our wealth and our wasteful habits will increase in parallel; they are beginning to look like insults to their poverty and to their dignity and will eventually spur them on to rise up in protest.

In Part II I underline and denounce not only this squandering and our privileged position but the increasing responsibilities of the rich countries, of the dominant economic systems – and particularly those of the rich and the powerful in the rich countries, who are no better than murderers snatching the proteins from the mouths of poor children. I give the private motorcar, the waste of paper, advertising and non-returnable packaging as examples of the type of abuses that heighten the poverty of the rest of the world. I point out that the fact that these privileges that take unfair advantage of our consumer society are becoming more widespread solely in the rich countries does not in any way justify their existence.

In Part III I show that in the face of our selfishness as 'haves' rather than 'have-nots', uprisings in the dominated countries are inevitable, since otherwise they are liable to be condemned to poverty in perpetuity. The 'rebels' would have to avoid atomic suicide on the grand scale but would aim to put an end to 'dominance' by looking for some form of national independence, by establishing a common front and struggling to revalue raw materials, to relinquish debts and nationalize the subsoil. They would thus lay the foundations for a single economic system for the whole planet . . . .

In Part IV I recommend that the rich countries should mobilize all their forces for Operation Survival and declare a state of emergency, and I put forward a series of 'Utopias' running parallel to those that I've outlined for the countries that have up to now been dominated. If arms were banned, incomes redistributed, taxes levied on energy and raw materials, scarce resources recycled and penalties imposed for owning private cars and urbanization there would eventually be new opportunities for agricultural expansion, if farmers could finally set their sights on plentiful supplies of food for everybody. And the seas would be protected and made international . . . .

In Part V we come to the toughest problems of all. It's no good simply calling for an end to dominance and injustice, for a halt to population growth; we would also have to find out *how* we can achieve this. And I see little hope of mankind avoiding terrible catastrophes. If we can single out those who are responsible, and create a 'new man' by throwing out all our current views on education, all this might help us to build a new society in which everyone would do his share of manual labour. For this we need a new set of morals, a new faith of the kind exemplified to a certain degree by China and Vietnam.

Finally, in my Conclusion I don't claim to have solved all the problems. I am far from happy with this essay – for that's what it is – in its present form, less so perhaps than with some of my earlier books. The studies on which it is based can and must be criticized. Some of the data they give, such as the

4

exact dates when our supplies of minerals will run out or when the level of pollution will become unendurable, are questionable if we take into account firstly man's inventiveness, secondly the possibilities for technological breakthroughs and thirdly the strength and durability of the biosphere and the ecosystem. But it would be highly dangerous for our future if we were led astray because we'd underestimated them. It's long been traditional among agronomists to prefer a counsel of caution, and I'm no exception. Before speaking out I've always backed up my views with hard facts. But then I really have plunged in head-first, as with the revolution in forage crops in France in 1947.

It would be irresponsible – in the literal sense of the word – to continue to ignore the one conclusion reached by the Club of Rome that seems to me irrefutable – the fact that exponential population and industrial growth cannot go on indefinitely, indeed cannot continue much longer in a finite world. It's perfectly possible to double industrial output in 10 years – the Japanese have done better than that. But to double it every 10 years for a whole century means multiplying production by a factor of 1,024. Over a period of 200 years . . . work it out for yourself! What are the material bases for this?

Even if some of the deadlines I've given turn out to be wrong, the time of expiry will still be so close that it's high time we drew up plans to find ways of avoiding it. At any rate, I believe that the categorical imperative of our age is to reduce social injustice, which is constantly on the increase and indeed has got worse in the last few years, particularly on the international plane. Patrick François writes:

> A historical analysis of economic development shows that in the early days the accumulation of private or state capital and the transition from a peasant economy to an industrial economy resulted in further inequalities. Properly planned development limiting these hardships is highly desirable.[2]

There is a danger that this 'first era' will last indefinitely in the dominated countries, unless we accept the fundamental modifications that will simply have to be made if we are to survive, and to cut back on injustice as far as possible. And in the last analysis a lessening of injustice is a precondition for our survival. We cannot reduce almost two-thirds of the world's population to a state of poverty which will worsen in some instances – this is what we are increasingly doing – without paying the price. There is a great danger that our failure to understand the situation will incite these nations to launch a series of dangerous revolts that will be stronger on violence than on organization. In that case our descendants will be the ones to suffer from our selfishness. Considering that warnings are coming at us from all sides, this selfishness of ours is beginning to look like the most enormous piece of stupidity in the history of mankind – which isn't exactly short on monumental errors.

Faced as I am with this situation, I cannot of course be so pretentious as to put forward, off my own bat, a Fourierist scheme for a 'new world' to go with the new man, Che's *el hombre nuevo* who is proving so difficult to train, particularly outside China, Vietnam and Korea. But I feel that from now on any of us who have examined some of these problems are morally obliged to do our bit to make our fellow-men throughout the world aware of the extremely serious situation in which we find ourselves.

The first step towards improving the likelihood of people accepting, in a rational way, that there is an urgent need for discipline on the material level (which in fact could well be compensated for very largely by greater freedoms) is to make them feel that they are taking part in a way of life that has been consciously chosen in the light of the highly acceptable constraints which will be necessary if our crazy species is going to survive. I say 'crazy' because we are the only species that is clearly capable of wiping out not only ourselves but all forms of life. And so an adventure which we can think of as unique in the infinite realms of the universe would come to a premature end!

The realists, or at any rate the best of them, point out that 'their' world is heading ineluctably for catastrophe. They therefore hand over to the Utopianists, who are called into the witness-box and as it were forced to look for ways to lay the foundations of various types of society which will have the lowest possible level of injustice and at the same time will be capable of survival. I have deliberately referred to the 'foundations' rather than the details of the organization, since it is early days yet to sketch in the details – and anyway they will have to be worked out on a majority basis. What we need to do is to set out a few relatively coherent ideas, a few plans that more often than not we shan't be able to put into practice until more people have grasped the situation.

That's why I've labelled this essay Utopian rather than

6

calling it a forecast or an advance report – not to mention a prophecy. I'm not sufficiently *au fait* with the art of telling the future to be able to do it successfully.[3] Which of us can boast of knowing how to prod people's consciences into action, with the possible exception of the Chinese (whose methods don't appear to be universally applicable)? Danilo Dolci tells us that we must do two things simultaneously: we must improve the species by rethinking our methods of bringing up children, and also improve the structures within which we live and act and realize our potential, transforming them just as they transform us.

Although I am fully aware that this essay is far from perfect, I hope the reader will understand that in view of my past actions I should not have been acting logically if I'd failed to speak out once I'd grasped the magnitude of the drama that will soon hit us, and the dominated countries in particular. Realizing that I wasn't sufficiently qualified to tackle the problems that confronted me, I hastened to consult several of my colleagues at the FAO in Rome (including Messrs Aubrac, Biro, Dudal, François, Malher, Perissé, Quaix and Saouma), once I had mapped out the general plan of my book and written the first draft. They gave me their own views, which were most valuable, together with a large amount of documentation. I also discussed these ideas with various personal friends (M. Szigeti, S. and O. Baffray and my wife), with the monks at the monastery of Saint-Benoît-sur-Loire; with Piganiol, Roland Pré and others at a group brought together at the Futuribles by B. de Jouvenel and A. C. Decouflé. Chaussepied, Chominot and Pluvinage, who were the other members of my group at the Agro, pulled my ideas to pieces – which was very helpful – and so on. Also, in April 1972 I had taken part in a discussion on 'Environment and Development' organized by Barbara Ward at Columbia University in New York.

It goes without saying that the responsibility for the text of this book is mine alone, but that doesn't mean that I shouldn't thank those who helped me.

I realize more clearly at this point that I have taken a considerable risk in thinking out some of the conditions for setting up a type of society that would be *less unfair* to the poorest among us and still *able to survive*. That was my specific aim and it seems to me essential that I should make this clear at the outset. I am fully aware of my own inadequacy and I therefore ask not for your indulgence (I don't show much indulgence myself) but for constructive criticisms, since without them we'll never get anywhere.

Part I

# THE FINAL DECADES OF
# THE WASTEFUL SOCIETY

1  *The unthinking optimists: Colin Clark,
Herman Kahn and Anthony Wiener*

In his book *Starvation or Plenty* Colin Clark,
who had led us to expect something better of him, recommends 'floating palaces at sea, using the land for agriculture
. . .' and says that 'very considerable economies could be
obtained if a large proportion of the population resided in the
colder climates, where the sacrifice of agricultural land would
have much less effect'.[1] My Quebec friends complain, in the
words of their *chansonnier,* 'My country is the winter.' And yet
Clark's actually suggesting they should go and live in the
Great North, or even Greenland! And he concludes by
quoting Malcolm Muggeridge: '. . . the whole universe is
about to be opened up, providing space to accommodate a
million, million times our present squalid little human family.'
Just work out the surface area of the globe, cover all the seas
with 'floating palaces' and the population he speaks of
wouldn't have enough room to stand upright, even if they
were packed in like sardines in a tin. He must be out of his
mind!

In their book *Year Two Thousand* Kahn and Wiener[2] speak
as economists and make forecasts, which they refer to as
absolutely foolproof, by simply extrapolating current production figures, expressed in money terms, without taking any
other factors into consideration. Their world is expressed
solely in dollars – an odd perversion, that. They therefore
state that by the year 2020 world production will have
increased by a factor of 5. By extending current growth curves
they calculate that by that date the Japanese will have an

9

annual per capita income of 33,000 dollars (1965 values), or in other words a family of five will have an *average* monthly income of over £6,000 – enough for each family to buy 3 *cars a month* with what they have left over after living very comfortably *and* handing over half their earnings to the taxman!

Their study makes no mention of physical limits, since wealth is measured solely in terms of current accounts. They do not take into account the fact that the acceleration that has taken place in Japan in recent years has been achieved at the expense of hospitals, roads, schools etc. and has created an unacceptable level of pollution.

Having tried in vain to find out what proposals they put forward for agriculture I turned to the index and looked under 'agriculture', only to find that the only entry under this heading read 'see manpower'. The one and only thing that interests them about the whole farming profession is the amount of manpower it will release for the other sectors! Mathematical extrapolations of this kind, without a grain of common sense, lead them to put forward a per capita figure of 3,000 dollars per annum in New Zealand in the year 2000, while the figure for East Germany is 8,300 dollars, for Indonesia 123 dollars and for Pakistan 200 dollars. They do not take into account relative population figures, natural resources or the possibility of redistributing incomes on a global basis.

When last heard of Kahn was calmly envisaging that by the second half of the twenty-first century 20 thousand million people would be enjoying an average per capita income of 20,000 dollars (1965 values). This means that there would be a world national product of 400 billion dollars – more than 100 times the present figure! Since he is not a stupid man we are entitled to wonder whether he is being sincere. After all, projections of this kind in effect justify continuing the increasing exploitation of the dominated countries, thus salving the consciences of the wealthy descendents of the Puritans in the United States, who are just as anxious to keep their consciences clear as they are to hang on to their wealth. So when the publishers give this book the subtitle 'A framework of speculation on the next thirty-three years' we can merely smile – and move on to more serious matters.

The French title of the Club of Rome's report is *Halte à la Croissance!* ('An End to Growth!'), which is stronger and less accurate than the English title, *The Limits to Growth*. The group of economists and scientists who worked on the report tried to take into account the implications for the future of the global ecosystem of 'five major trends of global concern – accelerating industrialization, rapid population growth, widespread malnutrition, depletion of non-renewable resources, and a deteriorating environment'.[3] They used mathematical models and complex computers to study the future development of these tendencies, the way they overlap and the consequences of the way they interact.

They do admittedly say that their model is 'imperfect, oversimplified and unfinished', yet they have no hesitation in warning us that:

> Furthermore, the basic behaviour modes we have already observed in this model appear to be so fundamental and general that we do not expect our broad conclusions to be substantially altered by further revisions . . . .
>
> Nevertheless, the vast majority of policy-makers seems to be actively pursuing goals that are inconsistent with these results.[4]

So they're pretty confident about their conclusions, which indicate in essence that unlimited growth of both population and industrial output, which is exponential and will therefore pick up speed all the time, will soon become impossible on our planet, since it is a finite world. This conclusion seems to me beyond all question, even without my having to 'consult' computers – after all their reply is always directly related to the data fed into them! Our Earth is like a spacecraft that has been launched into the universe and is quite simply under a blockade, with no reasonable hope that any other spacecraft will be able to come to its aid and lift the blockade. On the planetary scale we are condemned to 'rely solely on our own strength' and on our limited resources. In fact it's surprising that we've had to wait until the last few years for an awareness of this obvious fact to spread beyond a small circle of initiates – I hadn't been particularly struck by it myself!

If we accept the hypothesis that growth will continue, all the graphs worked out by the Club of Rome end up with the total collapse of the system during the twenty-first century. This collapse will occur because there will be dramatic shortages in food production, and most of all because we shall have created an unacceptable level of overpopulation and pollution. Let's have a look at these various threats.

### 3 'Non-renewable' resources

The fuels and minerals that we draw from the earth's crust are different from the products created by agriculture, fish-farming and forestry, all of which are renewed each season by means of a surplus of solar energy. If we assume that our usable mineral stocks are 5 times as great as those we already know about – the Club thinks this is an optimistic forecast – and that world consumption will continue to increase at the same rate as in recent years, we will have used up all our gold reserves in 29 years. (Don't forget that gold has industrial uses, though these were underestimated by Lenin, who wanted to cover the walls of our public lavatories with it!) By the same token we would have 41 years' worth of mercury left, 42 of silver, 48 of copper, 49 of natural gas, 50 of oil and zinc, 55 of aluminium, 61 of tin, 64 of lead, and so on. The only items that might last a hundred years are coal (150 years), iron (173 years), cobalt and chromium – but nothing would last as long as 200 years.

Figures like these have already been the subject of con-siderable controversy, and with reason. After all, we shall be able to use new ores, new products. But on the other hand it will become increasingly expensive to extract ores from deposits lying further beneath the surface. At the same time this will also use up more and more energy and, most important, will produce more and more waste matter and pollution. Must we rest our hopes for the survival of our descendants on hypotheses that cannot possibly be verified in the present state of our knowledge? Have we got the right to make bets on the future of mankind?

It's quite true that the extent of the oil reserves known to us has been increasing twice as fast as production in recent years. But they are increasingly being extracted from the seabed, which means that we are increasingly running the risk of polluting the seas. Now it appears to be absolutely essential that we should maintain life in the seas, from many different points of view. The only thing we can be absolutely certain about is that one day the supply of oil will run out. Every time we waste oil by burning up petrol in our cars for no particular reason we might do well to think of the youngsters in the Third World who are desperately short of proteins – of proteins that could be supplied by that very oil.

It is highly likely that our descendants living in the twenty-second century (I'm still hoping that there'll be some!) will be short of the resources of petrochemistry in their turn, yet these will be essential when the supply of ores has run out. This means that non-renewable wealth of this kind should be thought of from now on as the common heritage of mankind, worthy of being saved and cherished like the apple of our eyes! We shall have to work out a whole new policy for dealing with such resources. I shall be looking into the principles on which such a policy must be based later on. The rich and the powerful do not have the monopoly of our planet; it is the common property of all mankind, even though this idea may not be enshrined in Roman law or on the statute book.

4 *Poverty and the dangers of nuclear conflict*

The consumption curves that are forecast for these various models start from the supposition that the developed regions and the dominated countries will continue to be out of phase, and that the standard of living in the poor countries will never begin to resemble our own. All the projects initiated by the United Nations involve the idea that the inequalities current today will be maintained indefinitely. But if we take the opposite view and assume that the dominated peoples, those who belong to what is still known as the 'Third World', will also be in a position to enjoy the 'American' standard of living in 15 or 25 years' time (the length will vary according to their particular circumstances) – after all they've got just as many 'rights' as we have – our expectations as to the length of time the ores will last will be very much reduced; and

13

pollution would most probably reach a totally unacceptable level by the end of the century. Our hopes of surviving for rather longer now *rest solely* on continued poverty for the majority of our fellow-men, if our present structures are retained. A professor at the Collège de France, Raymond Aron, does admittedly think this a good thing, for he writes: 'Three and a half thousand million people *cannot* consume raw materials with the same voracious appetite as the Americans.' Well, yes, thank goodness their appetites *aren't* as voracious!

Our industrial output essentially turns on energy, with the non-renewable sources of energy – coal, oil and gas – providing 97 per cent of the energy used in industry. But the demand for electricity is increasing so rapidly that soon we won't be able to meet it from these resources, even if we add the potential of hydro-electric power. The United States plans to increase its electricity consumption by a factor of 3 – and probably by a factor of 4 – in 20 years. US citizens are already being asked not to use all their airconditioning appliances! In Japan the use of electricity has recently been expanding at the rate of 15 per cent per annum. If this rate of increase continues with compound interest for a hundred years the figures will be quite ludicrous, as present consumption levels will have to be multiplied by 117 million!

So until we are in a position to tap sufficient quantities of solar energy on an economic basis (when will that be, I wonder?) we must turn to atomic energy, which Barbara Ward rightly refers to as Prometheus' fire: 'We're playing with the raw material of the universe.'[5] What sort of dangers will our descendants increasingly be exposed to? Already we don't know how to get rid of nuclear waste safely, since some of it remains radioactive for a very long time. The people of Basle are successfully opposing a nuclear power-house that was to be built near the town.

The Americans insure against the danger that would be caused by an accident in this type of nuclear power-house to the tune of 560 million dollars. But the insurance companies refuse – rightly, from their point of view – to offer unlimited cover for accidents, as they do for shipwrecks. Some types of accident (and after all an accident is by definition unforeseeable) might bring about damage on a totally unimaginable scale. The Palestinians, Japanese and other revolutionaries who are prepared to die in bringing their cause to the attention of the world (remember the Munich Olympic Games in

September 1972) will no doubt be capable of damaging this kind of power-house . . . . Commoner tells us that a few slight cracks in the metallic sheaths surrounding the elements in which the caloric reactions are produced would be enough to set off radioactive irradiation.[6] So here we are deliberately running risks the extent of which we are quite incapable of gauging. Some of us at least can refuse to shoulder such a responsibility.

## 5 The increasing incidence of malnutrition and the 'Green Revolution'

In 1965-6, when I was writing my book *The Hungry Future,* I was accused of neo-Malthusianism because I had allegedly underestimated the potentialities of agriculture throughout the world. Some people produced dubious statistics to back up their claim that the countries with a high level of population growth were also increasing their agricultural output at a faster rate. Yet wherever I've looked into the question, I've always found countries – from India to Tunisia or Mexico – cheating systematically with their agricultural statistics – improving on them, in each case. And then we were told that the Green Revolution was going to break all records, sweep away all obstacles.

That was pushing it a bit. It's true that the potential output of Mexican wheat and Filipino rice is much greater than that of the traditional varieties. For the first time in the history of agronomy it can be claimed that tropical cereals can produce as much per hectare as in the temperate countries. But on the other hand these temperate cereals had been subjected to a careful process of selection more than a hundred years before Borlaugh began experimenting in Mexico in 1945.

But although these new varieties are more productive they are also more demanding. 'Miracle rice' can be grown success- fully only on absolutely level ground, where the water cover- ing it can be maintained at the optimum level for each phase of growth. In India, where most of the ricefields are watered only by the rain – which means not regularly enough – as well as the problem of levelling the ground a tremendous amount of work has to be done in the way of irrigation, draining and flood-protection. If water is to be controlled in this way at least 25 or 35 thousand million dollars will have to be invested.

On demographic grounds the development of the Ganges delta and Brahmaputra in East and West Bengal is a matter of urgency, more even than in China in the Middle Ages. This means that all the might of the West must be brought to bear, for the extent of the project is such that investment in terms of human labour, which would take care of the details of the development, is not enough. The West could still enjoy a clear conscience if it handed over with all speed – after all, people are dying of hunger – a *gift* of 10 thousand million dollars. As it would be a one-off payment this is in fact a ridiculously small sum compared to the 200 thousand million dollars (plus) spent annually on arms or the 20 thousand millions spent on advertising in the United States.

As this high-yield rice is smaller than the usual varieties the ricefields need to be weeded more carefully. And because it is irrigated it needs many more fertilizers, particularly nitrates. It also has to be treated very carefully against insects and disease. And a high level of technical expertise, plus heavy equipment and considerable reserves of manpower, are essential if it is to be cultivated successfully and the sowing can be done at the appropriate time. Other essentials are credit at non-extortionate rates of interest for obtaining new equipment, particularly fertilizers, and vast factories to turn out the fertilizers. Khrushchev insisted that from 1959 onwards the top priority for Soviet industry should be the production of fertilizers. Yet in 1973 their output is still nowhere near large enough and way below forecast levels; and the USSR is having to buy huge quantities of wheat.

All this makes it easier to understand why the high-yield varieties of rice accounted for half the ricefields in the Philippines in 1970–1 and 42 per cent in Pakistan, yet the figure in India was less than 15 per cent and in Sri Lanka (Ceylon) less than 4·5 per cent. In Sri Lanka, where at least 15 per cent of the existing ricefields are not used at the height of the rainy season, where the large-scale irrigation equipment is very much under-used, and where there is no shortage of land or water, more than 800 thousand people are still out of work, and in 1971 more than a third of the rice eaten in the country had to be imported. For the country was still living to a certain extent off the imperialist urge to give priority to crops that could be exported (tea, rubber and copra), though this didn't prevent the government from brutally crushing a revolt by young people whose aim was to modify the economic structures and hammer out a policy for achieving national independence. The fact that I have been speaking out against the socio-economic obstacles in the path of agricultural modernization for over 20 years hasn't unfortunately caused them to disappear.

After we'd been told that India would start exporting cereals in 1971 (like West Pakistan, which exported its poverty, in that its inhabitants couldn't eat enough because they didn't have enough money to buy food with) the forecasters had to climb down. *Le Monde* for 6–7 August, 1972 tells us: 'Famine is currently raging in six states of the Indian Union and is affecting 75 million people. At least 50 people are said to have died of hunger in just one of the 16 districts of Bengal.' This piece of news was held to merit a paragraph eight lines long, while in the same issue Bobby Fischer got seven half-columns! And most of the other French papers didn't even mention it.

I find it hard to imagine a famine on that scale, since in early 1959 I was stunned by the poverty in eastern Uttar-Pradesh, in what was allegedly a 'non-famine period'. In 1971–2 India harvested roughly 106 million metric tons of food grains, cereals and pulses (in 1970–1 the figure was 108 million), whereas the plans that I had seen on the drawing-board in India in early 1959 had forecast 110 million from 1966 onwards. Because of the unevenness of the 1972 monsoon they haven't even reached 100 million in 1972–3. Now the original objective as stated in the Plan was 129 million metric tons in 1973–4, though this was subsequently reduced to 122–5 million. Yet even this lower figure probably won't be achieved since, as the Food and Agriculture Organization (FAO) says in its 1972 report: 'The limited interest shown in the high-yield varieties and the fact that their effect on output has come to a standstill are worrying factors.' At the end of 1972 India was again importing 3 million metric tons of cereals, and 5 million in 1973. But still there was widespread starvation.

Whereas in 1969 China had 74 million hectares under irrigation, or two-thirds of its 109 million hectares of arable land, India was irrigating 37 million hectares out of a total of

138 million under cultivation, or more than a quarter compared with slightly over two-thirds. In 1973, 77 per cent of Chinese fields were under irrigation. What is more, India was doing it badly, wasting water on a scale that I referred to in my book *Lands Alive* as early as 1959–61.[7]

I can still see the frightened and dulled expression on the face of an eleven-year-old child I came across in the *zona da mata,* the sugar-producing coastal region of the Brazilian state of Pernambuco, near Recife. His hoe was far too heavy for his weak frame, which was more like that of an eight-year-old. And then there was the man living in the Agreste region a few miles inland who was quite willing to *sell* one of his thirteen children to get out of his terrible situation – and to get the child out.

If it seems difficult to be more specific, the World Health Organization tells us that approximately 150 million mothers and young children in the poor countries are suffering to various degrees from undernourishment and from advanced malnutrition – the main problem is lack of protein. Although the problem is worse in some cases than in others, in many instances it is serious enough to prevent their brains developing normally. Yet in spite of the enormity of this crime that is being committed every day, it doesn't even rate a mention in the 'news in brief' columns. In Recife the agronomist M. Mahler saw children fighting with dogs on the pavement in front of his house for the scraps left over from his own meals and the rubbish in the dustbins. He found this sight so hard to bear that he changed the whole direction of his research. The seriousness of these attacks against children's rights, which are completely disregarded, seems to me no less terrible than the summary executions and arbitrary imprisonments, or even the tortures, that are being inflicted on prisoners from Latin America to Iran, from Greece to Czechoslovakia and the Soviet Union . . . .


6 *The potential of agriculture is ultimately limited*


I agree with Samir Amin when the first thing he denounces in the underdeveloped countries is 'the machinery for impoverishing the masses, the way smallholders and artisans are being turned into a proletariat; the way the rural sector is being made semi-proletarian and the peasants grouped into village communities are being impoverished without proletarianization, urbanization and the massive increase in urban unemployment and in under-employment'.[8] But when he reminds us that underpopulated Africa cultivates only 170 million hectares, 'out of 1,400 million hectares of arable land in Africa south of the Sahara (land under crops, fallow land, pasture and forest land)', I should like him to look more closely at what type of land he's referring to, and at the type of climate.

The FAO calculates that in 1962 this 'intertropical' zone of Africa had 42 per cent of its genuinely arable land under cultivation, and this seems to me a more accurate assessment; it anticipates a figure of 52 per cent by 1985. The transition to continuous cultivation does involve some risks and many precautions need to be taken. In northern Senegal the shortening of the fallow period has lessened the supply of humus to soil that is already short on clay and too light. The loss of this binding agent has made it easier for the wind to erode the soil and to blow away the more delicate constituents, with the result that in the Kayor of Louga all that's left is an impoverished skeleton of coarse sand. It's true that rotation of fodder crops could make both continuous cultivation and the provision of humus possible. But for over 25 years agronomists have been trying in vain to get the Wolof peasants of Senegal to cultivate the land so as to be able to give better fodder to animals that bring them in so little, when they often go hungry themselves! As for the idea of forcing peasants to join state-run farms, this needs serious thought after the failures in the Soviet Union and Cuba.

Because the forests are receding and giving way to savannah, agricultural output in the regions directly concerned has already dropped considerably, whereas it could have been higher if acacias had been planted where the forest ends. The Sahara is spreading both to the north and to the south and its progress is being helped along by the nomadic shepherds, who are over-using the grazing land and thus degrading the vegetation to such an extent that it cannot always recover. Thanks to various types of erosion, the spread of the savannah and the desert and the drop in the level of humus in the soil, the value of our land heritage is decreasing with every day that passes.

In recent years the developed countries have stepped up their output by reducing the amounts of land under cultivation, but the poor and dominated countries have increased their production levels by extending the area under cultivation rather than by becoming more efficient. And they have achieved this by ploughing up land that shouldn't have been ploughed, 'entailing the permanent destruction of precious resources (pastureland and forest) for a relatively short-lived increase in the final level of agricultural output in regions that have turned out to produce poor crops', as the FAO's Provisional Indicative World Plan for Agriculture (1969) puts it.[9]

In May and June 1972 I was in the Central Atlas Mountains in Morocco, near Azrou, conducting a study into the village of Toufs-talt near Aïn-leuh. The Beni M'guild tribes lost part of their winter pastures because of colonization and then later they lost more of them to King Ranch, which is being farmed by an American company working with the State of Morocco. As a result they have been compelled to damage their high-altitude grazing land even more, with production levels dropping alarmingly as the land is over-grazed. In order to survive they have to plough steeply sloping land, and in doing so they take no precautions whatsoever against erosion, which would involve a great deal of extra work. Alexis Monjauze's experience of similar regions in Morocco and Algeria leads him to state that in 15 or 20 years erosion (water erosion this time) will have swept away all the arable land. Charcoal-dealers, who do very nicely out of this, egg on the foresters to authorize clear felling of holm-oaks over large areas, which again is liable to cause erosion. All the young people in the village hope for only one thing – to find work in France, which looks like Eldorado when seen from that distance.

Since Morocco gained her Independence in 1956 agricultural output has increased by about 2·2 per cent per annum, but the population has increased by 3·3 per cent. Malnutrition is on the increase among the poverty-stricken peasants, as their rate of under-employment rises. In Toufs-talt the means of production – land, water, draught-animals and livestock for income – are increasingly being concentrated among a small number of people. It's no good asking a *khammés*, a farmer who pays his rent in kind in the form of four-fifths of the harvest, to carry out work purely as an investment (measures to prevent erosion, irrigating equipment) without any pay, on land that doesn't belong to him. His wife weaves plaits of esparto-grass decorated with wool, which bring in about 1 franc a day, without her keep.

Far too large a proportion of the country's resources is earmarked for military expenditure, at the expense of agricultural and industrial modernization. And ever since Skhirat in July, 1972 and Rabat-Salé on 16 August, 1972 even the army no longer supports a regime that is too corrupt to survive much longer.*

The picture is equally grim wherever you look, from the wheat being cultivated on the precipitous slopes of the Andes in Venezuela to that on the hills round Agra in India. South of Agra land that once produced wheat has been too badly degraded to produce anything but millet and everywhere erosion is jeopardizing the potential output of the land. In a memorandum made after the Stockholm conference, A. Guérin, quoted by A. Sasson, who teaches in the Science Faculty in Rabat, Morocco, calculated that wind and water erosion had destroyed very nearly 2,000 million hectares over the last hundred years, or in other words more than the amount of land at present under cultivation. This seems a lot to me, but another estimate appears to be more realistic.

It has been said that between 1882 and 1952 15 per cent of ploughed land became unsuitable as farming land; 39·4 per cent had lost at least half its humus by 1952, compared with a figure of 10 per cent in 1882. Over these 70 years the proportion of 'good' land allegedly dropped from 85 to 41 per cent. All these data can do no more than offer an indication of the problem, but the extent of the damage cannot be underestimated. Since 1936 the United States has put very extensive protective measures into operation; so has China since 1950 and even more since 1958, though these have not always been sufficient. In the Soviet Union, where I saw some impressive ravines caused by erosion, Cheremisinov calculates that 50 million hectares are affected to a greater or lesser extent. In the United States the figure is still reputedly 10–11 million

* On 10 July 1971 a group of Moroccan generals attempted to stage a coup during a royal birthday party at the palace of Skhirat. Several ministers, generals and civilian officials were killed, as well as the Belgian ambassador, but King Hassan II was unhurt. On 16 August 1972 the king survived another highly spectacular attempted coup in which his plane was attacked by Moroccan Royal Air Force fighters (*translator's note*).

hectares, in spite of the enormous sums spent on soil-conservation.

Deterioration of this kind can be seen very clearly in a large number of places in southern France a few kilometres from Marseilles, on the road to Cassis, for instance, as well as all round the Mediterranean coast. There is similar damage in many places in Spain, which are being reafforested at vast expense, and even more in Greece, where the splendid forests of the ancient world have been replaced almost everywhere by bare rock, as for instance round Delphi . . . .

In the tropics laterization of the soil is producing damage that is often insidious but in some instances permanent, when erosion strips off the surface. Examples are the region north of the river Oubangui (near Bangassou, in the east of the Central African Republic), or the Kabré country north of Togo, where the villages are surrounded by a ring of ferric laterite that can be used to pave roads but has turned out to be incapable of supporting any vegetation whatsoever. When the bedrock of hard limestone is revealed by erosion in the Central Atlas region, the land is eventually used for stone quarries – but you can't eat stones.

The drop in the humus level is a very widespread pheno-menon, particularly in countries that do little in the way of soil-conservation and burn dried cow dung on their cooking fires, because they've got no other fuel once they've reclaimed their forests and put the land under cultivation, which is what has happened on most of the Indian plains. In ploughing up their grazing-land without compensating for this by intensive cultivation of fodder-crops they've made the shortage of fodder worse and have also reduced the productivity of their piteously emaciated cattle, of which incidentally they have far too many. The sacred cows are no longer producing enough milk to feed the children!

The FAO points out that the non-socialist developing countries (classed as Group C in United Nations jargon) could increase their arable land from 562 million hectares in 1962 to 660 million in 1985 and their harvested land from 385 to 519 million hectares. Here again the increase would be at the expense of grazing-land and a small amount of forest. It's true that if they copied the methods of the Chinese they could harvest an even greater area of land. The forecasts don't take into account the possibilities for mobilizing the peasant masses by firing them with enthusiasm – but then we've seen these methods fail in Cuba.

On 20 November, 1972 A. Boerma, Director-General of the Food and Agriculture Organization, stated that agricultural progress in the Third World was approximately 1 per cent instead of the 4 per cent forecast that year. This was the same figure as for 1971. He went into the question further by saying: 'We can think of a failure in one year as exceptional. But two failures in two consecutive years can no longer be seen as a temporary accident. The average target for the decade could be achieved only if successes way above the target (4 per cent per annum) were to be recorded; this would require an absolutely unprecedented effort in the last few years.'[10] Which means that failure in the agricultural sphere is already a certainty for the second 'decade of development'. In the underdeveloped countries per capita food production has been at a standstill since 1936! Enough of that! Then you'd also have to deduct from the area of arable land the 20 million hectares – the minimum – that would have to be removed from the 138 million hectares of ploughed land in India and reinstated as forests or permanent grazing-land, if we really wanted to protect our land heritage. And the $\frac{1}{2}$ million hectares – a conservative estimate – of marginal ploughed land to the south and on the hillsides of the Maghreb, from Morocco to Tunisia, that would have to be reconverted into grazing-land, and so on.

7  *Soon we'll be hit by a water shortage*

As an agronomist I know that we could greatly increase the output of the land now under cultivation – though we'll be looking later into the small print of such a move. The first method is irrigation. When badly organized, with not enough drainage, irrigation has led to alkalinity in some areas, and to salinity in the Nile Delta, and particularly in the Indus and Ganges valleys, where the efflorescence of salt has turned fertile soil into fields that are labelled *usar,* unusable – as in Perrégaux in Algeria.

Sasson states that 200 to 300 thousand hectares of land are lost in this way every year throughout the world. The use of tube-wells has made it possible for some of it to be desalinated and reclaimed, but only where there was good-quality water fairly near the surface.

Elsewhere, as in the Office du Niger* or in the Nile Delta, the underground water level close to the surface is rising and choking the soil, killing the orange-groves. Some of the dams in Algeria were blocked with silt that had been swept away by erosion before they'd even been put into use. In the Damodar Valley in Bengal, where I noticed in 1959 that an appalling amount of water intended for irrigation was being wasted, the farmers who used to farm land in the valleys that are now under water have instead sown their crops on the hillsides upstream from the dams. This has set off a process of erosion that will soon fill up the dams and thus cut back the forecast level of electricity output.

The reservoir attached to the Aswan Dam, of which Nasser had such high hopes, is filling up much more slowly than expected because the rate of evaporation has been higher than was predicted, and probably also because there has been persistent leakage. The Mediterranean coast, which was beginning to shift northwards because of silt, has been receding since the silt started to block Nasser's lake instead. Some of the land that can now be watered thanks to the new water-sources now available is made up of shifting sand dunes, and the failure of the state-run farms known as 'Al. Tahrir' or 'Freedom' to the west of the Delta suggests that little can be hoped from this.

When permanent irrigation is used more widely this creates only too often a parallel risk of a frightening parasitic disease, bilharzia. Men are not angels and many technicians who have over-specialized are more like sorcerers' apprentices. The facts about the global ecosystem are only just beginning to emerge in all their complexity, and we are trying to *dominate* nature instead of trying to join forces with her. We would admittedly aim to take as much from her as possible, but on the other hand we would respect her enough for her to be able to go on being of use to future generations. But this won't be as easy as has generally been thought up to now.

A large number of countries will even be running short of fresh water soon if the current population explosion and the

* An irrigation plant installed by the French near Segou in Mali; it is the only large irrigation network in French-speaking West Africa (*translator's note*).

equally explosive increase in urbanization encourages a matching growth in demand, which is already increasing 100 per cent every 15 years. Some of the orange-groves at Cap Bon in Tunisia are already having to go short of water because it is all going into swimming-pools for tourists, though it would have been perfectly easy to use seawater for this purpose, since the sea is so near. China supplies Hong Kong with water while Canada gives some of hers to the United States. A pipeline costing 100 thousand million dollars is planned. Why don't they draw up annual contracts – then the water can get more and more expensive!

The FAO's current forecasts predict that whereas in 1967 irrigation accounted for 70 per cent of the water used, 1,400 billion cubic metres, by the year 2000, even if the quantity doubled, it would use up only 51 per cent – because towns, industry and the mines would increase their consumption far more quickly. If the growth rate remained the same there would be a shortage of water by the year 2050, even if we managed to prevent the wastage that often occurs on an enormous scale in irrigation. The use of nuclear energy to desalinate seawater would only increase the problem of radioactive fall-out. It's no good going on thinking that unlimited progress continued indefinitely into the future won't ever bring great danger – after all, this isn't the nineteenth century!

8   *Fertilizers and pesticides: their uses and their dangers*

In the face of these constraints it would be legitimate to marshal all the tremendous possibilities for intensifying agriculture that we have already mentioned in connection with the Green Revolution. This potential would be even greater if we could shake off the yoke of a profit economy and mobilize the enthusiasm of the peasant masses. Yet if we were to seize more and more of the forest land in the intertropical zone in Africa and turn it into farm land, as they are already doing from Guinea to Zaire, from Kenya to Tanzania, aren't we liable to find that the soil is rapidly deteriorating because of leaching and erosion? We can already see this happening along the roads running across the Amazonas. According to R. Dudal, it is much more expensive to put new land into good shape than to intensify production on existing land. China recognized this fact as early as 1955.

When intensive monocultures are attacked by insects and disease they are protected by being treated with substances which may or may not be harmless – in many cases we can't be sure that they're not harmful. The spraying mixture used in the Bordeaux region contains so much copper that it is already damaging the vines. And everyone's beginning to get worried – especially since Rachel Carson's *Silent Spring* came out – about the possible consequences of using DDT all over the place and without due consideration, though it has of course been highly effective against malaria. But most important of all, if the poor countries continued to show a population increase at the forecast rate and insisted upon their right – which is after all a legitimate one – to eat slightly better, their demands would increase very quickly, according to the FAO's Provisional Indicative World Plan for Agriculture.

In 1985 they would need twice as many cereals and three or four times as much milk, meat, fish and eggs as in 1962. In 1975, half way through the Plan, we are way below the forecast rate. In fact what has happened is that instead of dropping by 33 or 40 per cent from 1975 onwards, as had been hoped, the proportion of people who are undernourished – either because they don't get enough to eat or because what they eat is of poor quality – probably stayed at roughly the same level in 1973 as when the Plan started, 11 years earlier. This meant that the *number* of people who didn't get enough to eat had increased in the same proportion as the global population figures. The FAO's report, being official, is more optimistic than some of the experts, and concludes that the number of people who are undernourished 'has remained constant at between 300 and 500 million'. The Plan asks for a 75 per cent increase in food in the 'developing' countries, or 3·8 per cent per annum from 1965 to 1980.

We are nowhere near reaching the necessary growth rate to achieve this, since in 1972 agricultural output was apparently 23 per cent up on the average for the period 1961–5, or 23 per cent in 9 years – which is a long way below 2·3 per cent per annum, with compound interest. The 4 per cent annual growth rate in the second 'decade of development' (1970–80) will clearly not be achieved, in view of the chronic shortages in Southern Asia (with a drop of 1 per cent in 1972) and the fact that many of the countries of Africa and Latin America are importing more food. In Chile this is even creating difficulties on the political front. Yet these consumption figures forecast by the FAO do not in any way imply that the poor countries would by then have caught up with the level of food consumption in the United States, or even with that in western Europe. There's an implicit belief that they won't be entitled to do so in 1985 or even in 2000, any more than they could in 1962.

This means, then, that it is generally accepted that a fundamental injustice is a permanent feature of our so-called civilization, a civilization that is in the process of collapsing, at that. All the poor will be entitled to is what they can afford after the rise – an extremely modest rise – that is forecast for their purchasing power. So the United Nations implicitly accepts as a fact that inequalities of this kind will continue and will increase. Now every time a calorie of vegetable origin is replaced in the diet by one of animal origin – say, a pork chop instead of potatoes – you need an average of 7 vegetable calories for 1 animal one. By American standards, the current level of agricultural output wouldn't produce enough to feed 1,000 million people! Cousteau reminds us[11] that industrial output would not produce enough to feed 600 million United States citizens.

The most important aid to agricultural progress is still the use of chemical fertilizers, either those that contain potassium or better still phosphates, or better still nitrates, along with an extremely small amount of a few other constituents, such as cobalt, copper or zinc. Up to 1850 the chief fertilizer throughout the world was natural manure. Down to 1950 this was still true for the majority of farmers the world over, and from 1950 to now it still holds good for the great majority of those. When I say natural manure I mean manure in all its forms, ranging from the night-soil used in Flanders or eastern Asia to the dungheap favoured by peasants in the West (which smells so good when it's properly prepared, as it is in Swiss villages). The municipal authorities channel all our excrement and urine into the sewage system – a practice that Victor Hugo condemned even in his day. The dungheap is still favoured by European farmers who have agreed to keep cattle – and have thus incidentally given up the possibility of a family holiday – in spite of the fact that our politicians, who prefer to listen to the cereal and sugar lobbies, have made no attempt to help the stock-farmers – hence our so-called shortage of meat, which is in fact highly debatable.

At the colloquium on the environment held at Columbia University in April 1972 my colleague M. Alexander of Cornell University made me leap out of my seat when he told me that in the United States poultry-breeders and cattle-breeders (each of whom owns thousands of birds or head of cattle) generally didn't bother to transport the mounds of manure produced by their animals to the fields and then bury it. It just wasn't worth the time and effort needed to move it, with salaries at their present level! So if it's more economic the manure is simply emptied into the local rivers, which then become polluted.

To make up for this wastage the use of nitrates is increasing at breakneck speed (from 326,000 metric tons in 1940 to 1,900,000 in 1965 and over 7 million in 1969). Without the manure it used to be spread with, the soil no longer receives humus, so it doesn't hold the artificial fertilizers as well. If huge quantities of fertilizers are used, as they are in the Netherlands, for instance, they are directed in increasing quantities into the underground water levels – which are then polluted all over again. This water is often supposed to be drinking water, but some of the nitrates are transformed into toxic nitrite. The same thing goes for the huge quantities of nitrates lurking in spinach that has been over-fertilized – so don't listen to Popeye!

I don't want to condemn the use of nitrates wholesale, because they don't present any danger if they're used properly and in moderation. The experts who advocate 'biological' agriculture are busy telling us to abandon all artificial fertilizers, but they don't say what they propose to do about the people who would have to go without food altogether – since more than a third of the world's population wouldn't get even the little they do today. It's been forecast that by 1975 the developing countries will have stepped up their use of of fertilizers from 2·6 million metric tons in 1962 to 14·5 million; by 1985 the figure is expected to reach 51·2 million. Yet in 1970 they were still using only 6·9 million, so they've fallen increasingly behind once again. If the target set by the FAO Plan is to be achieved the figures will have to have more than doubled in the 5 years to 1975. The Soviet Union is planning to buy vast quantities of fertilizers from the United States, in spite of the fact that it's still the second most important industrial power in the world.

In 1970 60 million metric tons of fertilizers were used throughout the world. Pawley's theoretical model for the year 2070 puts forward a figure 70 times larger: 'which would mean that the amount of chemical waste dumped in the lakes and seas would be 100 times the present level'. This would be totally unacceptable.

But after creating the most appalling erosion, particularly in the first decades of the twentieth century, the United States has been taking effective steps to combat it since Roosevelt's day. Are they now going to be equally serious in tackling the many types of pollution they are causing right now, once again on a higher level than elsewhere? This is probably the crux of the matter if it led them to rethink their entire consumer 'model' instead of praising it to the skies. But Barry Commoner[12] has shown that they're going to have to cut down on the use of nitrates because they've been too much of a good thing for the town of Decatur in Illinois, where what is supposed to be drinking water has far too high a nitrate content.

### 9 Air and water pollution: the frightening X factors

There are of course many other forms of pollution, and industry and the effluent from towns are responsible for a good deal more pollution of rivers, lakes and seas than agriculture. The state-owned French firm Potasses d'Alsace alone accounts for no less than 41 per cent of the salt that is dumped in the Rhine every year; the figure is 7 million metric tons of impure salt, all of which could be extracted and purified. Instead of presenting a threat to the soil and the water in Holland they could set up a large chemical industry, work the potash mines, which are not allowed to dump any more than they do at present, and take away some of the work involved in extracting salt from salt-marshes. They don't do any of this because it wouldn't be economically viable. Until very recently the law of profit didn't take into account the question of how best to safeguard our planet.

Every day now we're told that thousands of dead fish have been found floating belly upwards in such-and-such a river, polluting the atmosphere and the water. My grandfather, who was born in 1818, was a farmer and also carted logs at a place called Rubécourt, near Sedan. Whenever he took on a new farmhand in the years round 1850 the new man would insist on a clause being put in his contract to the effect that he wouldn't have to eat salmon on more than three days a week. In those days there was such a glut of salmon in the local streams at certain seasons that hardly anyone wanted to eat it – just look at the price of salmon today, which is of course affected by its increasing scarcity. 'If we haven't stopped salmon fishing in mid-Atlantic three years from now,' said Dorst in 1971, 'there won't be any Atlantic salmon to fish.'

Up to now industrialists have generally found it more economic to dump their waste matter in rivers, or even in the sea, than to purify it. They were more or less forced to do so by our profit economy – which did not take this kind of expenditure for social reasons into account – as otherwise they would be outstripped by their competitors. The French Committee for Regional Development calculated that between the Rhone delta and Menton there were 200 sewers polluting the Mediterranean – which explains why you're not allowed to swim on a large beach in Hyères. When a large number of people who had swum off the beaches near Rome during the summer of 1971 contracted viral hepatitis 600 Italian beaches were officially stated to be polluted.

Purifying plants are of course expensive. But the water they save could be used for irrigation, for which there is soon going to be a water shortage. It could even produce fertilizing elements of its own. In August 1972 Commander Cousteau reminded us that 'although few people realize this, the ocean is a miniature world whose resources are at least as limited as those of the land . . . it is extremely fragile and is completely at our mercy . . . . Five years ago the mass media popularized the idea that the sea's resources were inexhaustible, that its food supply was unlimited . . . . This crack-brained theory has now been knocked on the head, thank goodness.'[13]

Jean Dorst tells us that there are somewhere between 600

and 1,000 blue whales left, and 'with the 600 scattered throughout the seas of the Antarctic, we have reason to be afraid that the whole species may die out'.[14] In 1972 Japan and Norway refused to stop whaling. And Iceland justifies her case for extending her territorial waters by referring to the need to put a brake on the depredations caused by huge trawlers. Pollution is rapidly diminishing the potential of water, from Lake Eyrie, which contains no form of life at all, to the Baltic Sea, which has no oxygen on the sea bed. The North Sea and the northern Atlantic will soon be further casualties of pollution. The phosphates in detergents encourage the growth of algae, which then use up all the oxygen that has dissolved in lakes, to the detriment of the fish, and so it goes on. First the rivers get polluted, then the lakes, the estuaries, the inland seas and eventually the high seas.

Once all these different areas of water have been polluted it's the turn of the air, which is after all the source of all life. It used to be thought that the supply of air was inexhaustible and that it had no market value – but that was when it was fit to be breathed. When 5,000 people died in London in 1952 from the effects of smog, which had been a deadly scourge since the nineteenth century, the London County Council, which had more real power than its counterpart in France, took measures against the smoke and soot. As a result the sky over London is already beginning to look a bit bluer – which shows that it can be done, at any rate if industrial output and the use of cars and fuel continue at the present rate. The schoolchildren of Tokyo, which is rapidly turning into a gigantic megalopolis, are beginning to suffer, and on some street corners you can increasingly see the local cops – those pillars of our civilization – gulping down huge dollops of oxygen from special oxygen-posts. Some astute salesmen are even wondering whether they couldn't manage to persuade the people of New York to buy containers of compressed air from Alaska!

Lead will soon be in short supply, yet it's being pumped out into the atmosphere to improve the performance of our private cars, which are responsible for a good 25 per cent of all air pollution. It's been estimated that thanks to the motorcar there are already 300,000 metric tons of lead floating about over Europe. Sulphur dioxide is harmful to the lungs, while particles of dust and rain can cause calcification of the pleura, and carbon dioxide decreases the supply of oxygen to the tissues by combining with the haemoglobin. In his book *Closing Circle: The Environmental Crisis and Its Cure* (1972) Barry Commoner gives a detailed account of the various phases that resulted in the pollution of the air over Los Angeles and the way the local council is fighting the giants of the car industry. But he doesn't recommend the most effective solution, which would be to ban private cars altogether and replace them by public transport.

The Japanese are beginning to export their pollution and their most asphyxiating industries by setting up steel-works in Singapore and lending capital to the people of Perth and Brazil so that they can treat their minerals on the spot. If these industries were distributed more evenly, they could admittedly make a useful contribution to the development of the poor countries – provided they were no longer an instrument of economic or even political domination, as they are within our present structures.

I won't say any more about this type of pollution, as I don't know very much about it; I'm told that it's not an easy point to make up one's mind about. It has certainly proved possible to divert the sewers that used to dump their effluent in Lake Annecy, and air pollution can be reduced, though the cost of the operation will soon escalate if we want to come anywhere near preventing it altogether. But it seems to me that the worst danger of all is the increasing amount of carbon dioxide in the air. The figure apparently increased by 14 per cent from 1830 to 1930 and is now increasing at the rate of 0·3 per cent per annum. When the figure is double that for 1860 – which should be at the beginning of the twenty-first century if the increase continues at the same rate as our industrial 'growth' – irreversible changes may well occur in the climate. The reason for this would be that the excessive proportion of carbon dioxide would create a hothouse effect and thus overheat the atmosphere. At the same time, if the end of an ice age brought about a natural cycle of reheating the ice at the two poles would melt – don't forget that it hasn't always been there – and the level of the oceans could rise by about 60 metres, drowning Paris and all the coastal plains in the world; the intertropical climate would then become unbearable. It's no longer good enough to say that we're not in a position to state positively that a catastrophe of that magnitude will occur. It would be better to make sure that we are in a position to state positively that we will not help to bring the date nearer – which calls into question our 'religion' of growth at all costs.

Don't let's bring up for the moment the question of pollution by refuse. The people of New York create 1 metric ton of refuse per head per year, and they don't know what to do with it. The French, being less disciplined in such matters than many other nations, dump their refuse all over the place, or in some cases collect it from outlying parts of the countryside and burn it, whereas a large amount of organic waste matter could be used as fodder or to enrich the soil with humus. The traditional peasant class knew how to recycle their waste matter, but nowadays the canals are more like cesspools where they run through towns, the hedgerows are stuffed full of plastic bags, and rubbish dumps are springing up all over the place, round picturesque little villages in Tuscany, for instance. All this suggests that the world of tomorrow will be increasingly repellent, for as plastic is not bio-degradable nature cannot reclaim it.

But one thing we can be sure of: we are systematically throwing our fragile system off balance. Any attempt to fight chemical pollution involves the use of energy, and therefore increases the level of thermic pollution. So we're in the process of unleashing a terrible self-supporting phenomenon, a vicious circle, and we're not at all sure where it's leading us. Now I'm still one of those who like to see things as they really are, having done my bit to warn people for many years and retaining a sense of responsibility. I prefer not to take part in the type of unconsidered actions that our leaders embark on so lightheartedly, with Émile Olivier in 1870 foreshadowing Michel Debré, French Minister of Defence, in 1973, with his pro-nuclear policy and his programme to encourage a rise in the birth-rate. For we haven't yet looked at the most appalling, and possibly the most imminent, of the swords of Damocles that our leaders are cheerfully holding over our heads, whether they do so unconsciously or to gratify their sadism.

Those who allow man's common heritage to run down in this way, whether they are business firms or individuals, are quite simply stealing from our collective wealth. In some cases the extent of the theft is greater than the extra profit levied on the worker, or even on the consumer.

For many years American officials denied that there was any danger from nuclear tests and radioactive fallout. Then in 1959 the British noticed that the amount of Strontium 90 and Caesium 137 in their atmosphere was increasing; both of these are highly dangerous and they last for 28 and 30 years respectively. So the Russians and the Americans realized that it would be better, in their own interest, to negotiate a nuclear test ban in the atmosphere. China and France refused to sign the treaty and are continuing their tests. We are right to protest about this, though we shouldn't forget that the prime responsibility rests with the United States and the Soviet Union, who between them have accumulated enough nuclear material to wipe out the whole of the human race many times over.

According to A. Sasson, 'By early 1972 the United States had exploded 188 devices in the atmosphere and had made 351 tests underground; the figures for the Soviet Union were 142 and 112; for France 30 and 13; for Great Britain 21 and 4; for China 11 and 1.'[15] And to think we used to laugh at our ancestors for worrying in case the sky fell on them! In fact they were more far-sighted than our leaders!

The cost of manufacturing atom bombs is dropping rapidly. Robin Clarke calculates that each bomb costs 300,000 dollars, or even 150,000 'if they are mass-produced .... For 300 million dollars a nation could at least afford to conjure up the nuclear spectre.'[16] Perhaps one of these days nuclear weapons will be sold commercially, as other weapons are. The greatest danger if nuclear energy becomes more widespread is that an increasing number of countries will be able to make their own.

It's not so long ago since the death of Hitler, and even Stalin, who would have lost less sleep over the use of nuclear weapons than other people (though actually it was Truman who started it!). We've also been told (somewhat late in the day) that Lin Piao was a dangerous man. Imagine what a successor to Papa Doc Duvalier or President Trujillo could do with a bomb of this kind if they suddenly went mad – or even the Greek colonels, though this doesn't perhaps apply to them because they've got too many people breathing down their necks. Some of us might feel alarmed at the thought of a man like Bokassa or Adim with this type of weapon at their disposal; and what about Somoza, Vorster or Stroesser – I mention them purely as examples – or even some general or other in Brazil, or Indonesia, or Thailand....

Although a whole network of precautions has been set up we can't disregard entirely the possibility that a whole series of operators (cf. Dr Strangelove) may suddenly go raving mad, or at any rate be driven by overweening ambition to commit an act of madness. Once again the survival of mankind is at the mercy of a series of hypotheses – and this time the danger is closer. This means that our survival is saddled with a series of huge mortgages of a kind that previous generations never knew. The genocide and biocide that are at last coming to an end in Vietnam are concrete realities to which the reasons adduced by the Nuremberg trials can be applied. It's a pity that the only people who are accountable for their crimes are those who are defeated hands down, as the Nazis were.

There's no consolation in the fact that, thanks to un-provoked attacks of this kind, we'll soon be able to measure with a greater degree of accuracy the damage that can now be done to harvests, forests, flora, fauna and most of all to man himself. Nor is it any help to know that the French Com-mission on the Pacific, which is in charge of nuclear ex-plosions, has embarked on a thorough examination of the biology of Mururoa Atoll in Polynesia before and after the tests. And since they voted for Nixon, the majority of ordinary American citizens agreed to the bombing of the dykes in North Vietnam (incidentally French engineers helped to strengthen them right down to 1944, and I myself walked up and down them many times between 1929 and 1932).

From now on nuclear weapons represent the most serious threat of all. But this doesn't mean that we shouldn't condemn the increasingly terrible conventional weapons that the United States are constantly 'perfecting' in Vietnam. They deserve our condemnation for many different reasons. They bring ruin to the poor countries and at the same time contribute dangerously to the growing shortage of natural resources. For instance, they are one of the major reasons for the rise in the annual consumption of copper from 1·6 million metric tons in 1950 to nearly 7 million in 1970.

Whereas the price quoted for copper rose steeply from 1963 to 1967/8, the timely drop in the price was a serious setback to Allende's experiment in Chile; similarly, the drop in cocoa from 1963 to 1966 compromised Kwame Nkrumah's efforts in Ghana. But these things aren't always a coincidence. France could not manage to balance her foreign currencies without her sales of arms to countries all over the world, including South Africa. A large number of the Third World nations, particularly India and Pakistan, though this is also true of Egypt, Peru, Algeria and Morocco, are having to sit by and watch their development being seriously threatened by military expenditure, which comes on top of the huge sums squandered by the civil service.

The annual figure of 180–200 thousand million dollars that is spent on arms all over the world represents an appalling waste of the best ores, but it also wastes the world's best brains. Both in France and in the United States most of the public funds allotted to research goes to the military. The results of this research are never published, because they count as strategic secrets. This hinders the progress of the basic sciences, which are after all becoming increasingly indispensable if we are to survive. Yet our survival depends on devoting the most essential part of this type of research to it.

If the public money that is being squandered on military expenditure were instead transferred to the countries of the Third World it could have a decisive effect in speeding up their development. The manpower and the plant that would be freed by a ban on arms production could be used to manufacture the equipment that the Third World so badly needs. But convincing those responsible is easier said than done. They aren't totally insensitive to the pressure of public opinion, but they know only too well how to manipulate it, thanks particularly to the devilish invention of television. Our only hope now is that they too (or rather their descendants) will scent the danger.

In *The Science of War and Peace,* Robin Clarke paints a terrifying picture of the way the military and industry have joined forces (Eisenhower exposed this complicity between them) to stage a takeover – no other word for it – of space research, the race to the moon, the possibilities for putting nuclear bombs in orbit and even the world's oceans:

The US Navy currently spends about $2,100m. a year on applied research and development . . . . The pace of oceanographic research is largely controlled by the military . . . . In a saner age it would be unthinkable that most of our knowledge of 70% of the Earth's surface could be locked up in the confidential drawers of the world's military establishments.[17]

Barry Commoner is also worried about the kind of world we're going to leave our children.

To kill 72 per cent of the United States population about 120,000,000 people): 500 10-megaton bombs dropped on centres of industry....
To burn all vegetation on 50 per cent of the United States land area: an attack of about 7,500 megatons of weapons ....
To destroy by fall-out radiation the usefulness of 91 per cent of United States crop-land and to destroy 95 per cent of hog production, 94 per cent of milk production and 88 per cent of all cattle: an attack totalling 23,000 megatons on combined military and population targets.[18]

And Commoner then asks a truly basic question: 'Could the population recover?' The answer is by no means certain. Anyone who envisages the possibility of a nuclear war is simply being irresponsible.

When you read this type of statistic about a territory as vast as the United States, the 'deterrent force' of a tiny little country like France, pointed 'in all directions' (i.e. against all objectives), as those responsible for it put it, seems the most frightening threat of all, the biggest obstacle to our own chances of survival, the greatest piece of folly imaginable. France's tests in Polynesia have rightly been condemned by the countries bordering on the Pacific, from New Zealand to Japan and Peru.

11 *Zero growth in the world's population must be achieved as soon as possible – starting with the rich!*

We are always being given carefully doctored statistics to prove that the current population explosion – and today's figures completely contradict all pre-1945 forecasts, which drastically underestimated the extent of the problem – cannot be reversed for many decades. Even if a large-scale family planning campaign were adopted in the near future and each

37

couple had an average of two children the growth-rate would not decrease, and so on. But is an average of two children really necessary? I am more concerned about the persistent campaigns to step up the birth-rate, in a country such as France for instance, where some people are rash enough, or should we say brash enough, to put forward a target of a population of 100 million. At the same time they're trying to slow down the population growth in Reunion Island, where the unemployment figures are a serious threat to social stability in the years to come, as they are in all the dominated countries.

The first question to be answered is: when will the majority of world opinion really grasp the seriousness of the threats to our planet? In 10 years' time it will already be very late in the day to envisage putting into effect the series of bold and decisive measures that are absolutely essential. And the most essential discipline of all is that of birth control, if we want to avoid a degree of austerity that would be very hard to accept. If genuine political and social discipline prevails, as in China or in North Vietnam, the birth-rate falls fairly quickly, even in rural areas off the beaten track.

The birth-rate does also drop when a degree of affluence is reached, as in Hong Kong or Taiwan, or even in South Korea (though I didn't see much sign of affluence there). But there is little likelihood of a situation like that arising in most of the dominated countries.

It would be just about possible, particularly when methods of contraception and abortion have been improved, to keep the birth-rate down to the same level as the death-rate, and thus bring about zero growth in a short time. This would involve the introduction of authoritarian measures – though they would surely be justified in view of the global danger we are facing. But to make them acceptable a totally different international climate would have to be created from the present system of dominance, which places a crippling mortgage on the shoulders of the poor countries. They would first have to be freed from this dominance, then educated.

Some of the Americans who set out to preach birth control in the dominated countries – incidentally making no distinction between overpopulated India and the underpopulated Amazon basin, between tropical Africa and the Middle East – do so in good faith. But the shrewdest of them see this as a way of maintaining their hold over such countries, since increasing poverty may well be a prime cause of revolt. In stressing the dangers the Club of Rome does not lay enough emphasis on the fact that pollution and the dwindling supplies of ores are not caused by the poor nations, but are first and foremost created by the rich nations.

Don't forget that although the United States represents only 6 per cent of the world's population, in recent years it has wasted (a more accurate term than used up) 42 per cent of the global consumption of aluminium, 33 per cent of the copper and oil, 28 per cent of the iron, 26 per cent of the zinc and silver, 25 per cent of the lead, 26 per cent of the tin and so on, plus a good half of the natural gas. But we pay for everything we use, they say. Yet they don't specify how they pay for it. The Chileans have shown that there is a huge discrepancy between their investments in real terms and the profits they get from their copper mines. They have recently found it easier to pay for what they buy from foreign manufacturers in counterfeit money (by issuing more than 60 thousand million dollars' worth of banknotes guaranteed for 10 thousand million dollars and virtually forcing the central banks to accept them). Only the small-scale forgers, those who are mere craftsmen, are penalized by the law. In his *Threepenny Opera* Brecht showed how his thieves turned themselves into bankers .... He was clearly a man ahead of his time!

Since ores are soon going to become scarce the world is virtually in a state of siege. This means that it is essential not to organize things solely on the basis of market forces. If we showed more concern for social justice and survival, the threat of worldwide shortages should soon force us to introduce a global rationing system whereby scarce resources would be allocated on the basis of genuine need. The first thing to go would be armaments. The rich nations, whose population represents only 29 per cent of the total population on the planet, consume – or rather waste – over four-fifths of the world's resources. They won't find it easy to accept a drop in what they somewhat oddly call their 'standard of living' – which includes a figure for arms production! Yet since they are the chief culprits as far as waste and pollution are concerned, if they are really worried about the world's survival they should be the ones to set the example of self-discipline in birth control. After all, 200 million Americans pollute more than 5,000 million Indians would.

We can't go on relying on family planning on its own, since this merely prevents the birth of unwanted children. We can't go on entrusting the survival of mankind to the good nature of such a large number of more or less irresponsible procreators. Now that we have at last begun to realize how limited our resources are we are entitled to think of those who encourage a rise in the birth-rate as at best oblivious to the danger, or at worst power-hungry criminals. This means that it is going to be increasingly necessary to introduce authoritarian measures designed to lower the birth-rate. But they will never be accepted unless they start with the rich nations and involve educating the other nations. The custom whereby girl babies born to poor families in China were abandoned can therefore be seen, in the light of recent observations, as a reasonably wise move, as can the systematic practice of abortion in Japan both before 1869 and after 1945. The moralists among us who disapprove of such measures should start by condemning war and their own overconsumption.

As early as 1931 I stressed the urgent need to cut the birth-rate in North Vietnam and I repeated my warning in my first book, *La Riziculture dans le delta du Tonkin*. When G. Wéry presented this book to the Academy of Agriculture in 1935 he felt compelled, since he was a good Catholic, to make certain reservations about my suggestions for birth control. In 1971 the Catholic Union of French Scientists 'warned Christian consciences against an attitude towards conception that represents, in the present situation, a form of individualism . . . . It is becoming impossible to think of procreation solely in terms of a personal decision and personal morality.'

Yes, but the gap from 1931 to 1971 represents forty wasted years, during which the population explosion occurred on a scale that has jeopardized the very future of mankind. During those forty years both communists and Catholics generally rejected the very idea of neo-Malthusianism. And in summer 1972 the Moscow *Pravda* launched a new campaign to raise the birth-rate, while in that very same year the Soviet Union, a huge but underpopulated country, imported 18 million metric tons of wheat, an altogether unprecedented figure! As for the Japanese, they're actually experimenting with bonuses for extra children . . . .

When France and the rest of Europe eventually manage to grasp how serious the situation is – and the sooner they do so the easier it will be to make the necessary changes – their first move, once incomes have been levelled out, will be to cancel all tax advantages and housing subsidies, and in particular all family allowances, for those with more than two children. The heads of small working-class families in Montargis tell me that they're fed up with paying out for their idle neighbours who live off their children.

The United States will have to go even further and tax large families increasingly heavily, particularly the very rich families, who are the most wasteful of all, real vandals. Then later they'll have to fix strict quotas. Once the rich nations have really got to grips with the problem of cutting the birthrate we'll be in a better position to recommend the same policy with some degree of effectiveness to the countries where it's needed most – which means from the Maghreb to southern Asia and the Far East, with special emphasis on Egypt, Pakistan, India, Bangladesh, Java, North Vietnam and southern China. The process of rationing scarce resources should then be based on the population figures for each country in 1985. Any increase above these figures would not entitle them to a supplementary allowance. In China there is no clothing allowance at all for a third child.

12 *The difficulties posed by population shifts – a necessary evil*

At the same time the problem of the present distribution of the world's population should be examined, since it is the basic cause of injustice in the world today. The economic expansion of the United States, South America and the South Sea Islands in the nineteenth and twentieth centuries could never have occurred if it hadn't been for the huge wave of immigrants from Europe, which was swelled by a propaganda campaign that was sometimes deliberately misleading. There are large numbers of Russians in Siberia, of Chinese in South-East Asia and Africans who were moved to the American continent against their will. Huge numbers of Indians have emigrated to Ceylon, to the Caribbean, to Guyana, Mauritius, South Africa and East Africa (where a new form of racism resuscitated by men ranging from Vorster to General Amin is making life very difficult for them).

41

It's true of course that these 'migrations', particularly in the countries with temperate climates, in fact represented a conquest by the White Man, who did not show the remotest interest in the welfare of the 'natives'. Then later on it would be more accurate to speak of African slaves, or Indian semi-slaves, being deported. But other types of immigration even more humane than the recent influx of African immigrants to western Europe are perfectly possible. There are also ways of legally preventing certain types of exploitation by colonizers, whether they be white, yellow or brown, without having to label them 'racist'.

Yet just when this global population mobility seems to be most necessary restrictions on all such movements are becoming more and more marked. Racism is still present in countries such as Britain or France that often claim to be more civilized than the rest of the world. The recent clampdown on immigration is designed to restrict entry to the rich countries to the better educated. This has the unfortunate effect of depriving the backward countries of their very small number of well-educated citizens. This brain drain is just about as costly for the dominated countries as the economic depredations they are being subjected to.

The United States is planning to stop cultivating roughly 30 million hectares of land, and 20 million hectares has recently been filled in. In western Canada a system of bonuses designed to cut the area of land under wheat by half has just been introduced. In Australia the production quotas for milk, sugar, wheat, eggs etc. represent a whole series of Malthusian measures that will be even more necessary in the near future as a result of Britain's entry into the Common Market. Considering the huge natural potential of these vast tracts of land it is totally unjust to restrict their immense wealth to their present small populations – their population density is way below the global average. Such injustice is unacceptable, particularly in view of the tragic prospects for the future.*

Your expectation of life is fixed for ever, within narrow limits, by the place where you happen to be born – India or the United States, for instance. Tropical Africa and Latin America are said to have been depopulated, and so they have on the whole. But southern and eastern Asia, from Egypt† to Java,

* Since I wrote this, all these restrictions have been lifted (*author's note*).
† I've grouped Egypt with Asia because her demographic situation is very similar (*author's note*).

from India to China, from Bangladesh to Vietnam, are tragically over-populated. Indonesia alone is in a position to restore the balance within her national frontiers, by moving people towards Sumatra, Irian in New Guinea, Borneo and the Celebes. If the crowded Javanese, packed in like sardines, knew that rice would definitely fetch higher prices in Sumatra they'd be more willing to move there. Why shouldn't the surplus populations in Asia – provided they aren't increasing – slowly move out, at a reasonable pace and as transport permitted, to Siberia, the South Sea Islands, America and Africa? Asian immigrants could be offered jobs clearing the areas earmarked for development, but they should not be allowed to trade, as they soon start exploiting the Africans.

If the number of Japanese immigrants to Brazil had continued after 1930, though at a steadier pace, her agriculture and economic development could have gone ahead by leaps and bounds once again. And this new upsurge in development could have overtaken the manufacture of luxury articles for minorities already enjoying a privileged status; these cover an excessive proportion of the present rate of growth and may well soon start to slow it down. In view of this I should have preferred to see General Amin forcing 'his' Ugandan Asians to turn to jobs that are directly productive, by becoming self-employed craftsmen or entering family businesses or farming, or even becoming teachers or doctors, instead of simply expelling them – a racist act, as Julius Nyerere rightly said.

Having tried to indicate the extent of the threats hanging over the future of mankind and the constraints they are increasingly forcing us to accept, I must now point the accusing finger at those who are chiefly responsible for this situation. It's no longer good enough to make a general proclamation to the effect that, as in the titles of two of the books I quoted at the beginning, we must 'put a stop to growth' and we must 'change or disappear'.* We still have to identify those for

* The titles French publishers give to translations of British or American books on ecology, the environment and pollution tend to be more dramatic than the originals. The reference here is to the Club of Rome's *The Limits to Growth* and the *Ecologist*'s *Blueprint for Survival*, which appeared in France under the titles *Halte a la Croissance!* and *Changer ou Disparaitre?* respectively. Similarly, Barry Commoner's relatively sober title *Science and Survival* becomes *Quelle terre laisserons-nous a nos enfants?* ('What sort of a world shall we leave our children?') (*translator's note*).

whom it would be more logical and fairer to halt growth, and to state where and in what areas of production this should occur. The idea would be to make growth easier by means of better organization in the places where it is still an essential weapon in the fight against a level of hunger, poverty and ignorance that will be increasingly unacceptable from now on.

If we want to avoid disappearing from the earth altogether we'll have to change our way of life and the basic concepts underlying our civilization, starting with our system of appropriation and management of production. But who are the people for whom this change is most urgent, and where, and how? The Club of Rome and the British *Ecologist* group seem to have set themselves the task of dealing with these vast and complex problems more or less 'apolitically' – as if they could! In fact they're suffering from a dangerous delusion, because any attempt to be apolitical masks a feeling of complacency towards our current political structures in relation to the matter in hand. Such an attitude is therefore ultimately conservative. If we want to avoid the terrible catastrophes that now threaten us all (or at least the descendants of the oldest among us) in the medium term, we must first work out who or what is responsible for the unacceptable wastage of resources that is leading us on the road to ruin. This is our only hope of survival.

I shall therefore attempt to unravel some very knotty problems, though I shan't be able to solve them all. I may perhaps be forgiven for any shortcomings, since I'm working alone, without computers – though even computers can reply only in terms of the data fed into them, which explains why they misled McNamara about the date when the Vietnam War would come to an end. McNamara's now trying to redeem the 'sins' he committed in Indochina by asking the World Bank for more aid for the Third World, for greater consideration to be shown to the poor in the Third World countries and for more attention to be paid to the problem of employment (22 September, 1972). I'm afraid he'll soon have to go even further if he wants to go up to Heaven!

But the situation is so serious that anyone who thinks he has something to say must speak out, and quickly, because time is short. If we want to get a clear picture of what's to be done we must stage a confrontation between those who hold different and even conflicting viewpoints. I shall first of all emphasize what seem to me to be the most dangerous mistakes, since these are the ones that must be put right most quickly. I shall show that this will be possible if we break right away from our present economic structures. A reforming zeal can be useful as a first step, to speed up people's awareness, but it won't be enough.

The poor countries will no longer accept our economic dominance over them, since this robs them of their mineral resources and prevents this zone of 'fringe capitalism' from entertaining any real hope of developing. But who exactly is responsible for the drama that is hanging over all of us?

Part II

# THE RICH PEOPLE IN
# THE RICH COUNTRIES
# ARE TO BLAME

1   *The profit economy can never bring growth to
a standstill*

In an economy dominated by market forces
the value of products, provided there aren't too many
monopolies, is more or less determined by the law of supply
and demand. This is a good thing in one way in that it
encourages manufacturers to take consumers' requirements
into account – we've seen the difficulties Cuba encountered
when she tried to free her economy more or less completely
from consumer requirements. Yet this type of economy takes
into consideration only those consumer demands that can be
fulfilled, and thus ends up by creating an increasingly unfair
global distribution of income, since the poor can hardly ever
express their requirements. And nor can the needs of the
community as a whole be expressed, which means that the
needs of the community, of the infrastructure (roads, airports
etc.), of education, health and ecology – in short the requirements for survival – cannot always make themselves felt. And
it's the capitalists who 'direct' demand.
So the economic machine is liable to run amok in favour of
the rich, to concentrate increasingly on non-essential activities
– which restrict its field of action and at the same time put
more people out of work. This is particularly true of the
dominated countries, especially South America. This type of
system totally fails to recognize the right of everyone to work
and to enjoy a decent standard of living. Yet these rights are
both more important and more urgent than the right to vote,
which can so easily lead to various forms of corruption.
Finally, the profit-earning capacity of the capital owned by

47

firms that are subject to the law of the jungle and are forced to compete depends absolutely on ongoing exponential growth. But this will soon lead us into global catastrophe, according to the specialists we've just quoted. When demand falls our capitalists, who are also on the lookout for profits, try to create artificial demand by means of advertising. I shall be going into the abuses inherent in this method later. It involves things such as deodorants for men, which are quite stupid and even dangerous (because they prevent beneficial perspiration and thus lead to neuroses and the use of tranquillizers that can be bought over the counter).

Who are the chief culprits in the rush to waste scarce resources? The rich countries, of course. We've already seen what's happening in the United States. But the European countries are a good deal to blame as well, in that they're attempting to take up the famous 'American challenge'. And within these developed countries it's the people with the money and the power who waste most. It's odd to see how the specialist press woos ordinary working people, whether they're manual workers or shopgirls, salaried staff or secretaries, not by interesting them in the major issues of the day or in matters that affect them directly, but with the love-life and general goings-on of film or television stars and millionaires.

A man like Aristotle Onassis can gratify far more desires than Louis XIV ever could, because he has hundreds of slaves to look after his luxury activities – domestic servants, interior decorators, yacht-builders, car and aeroplane manufacturers, suppliers of various kinds, such as those who send him his weekly supply of lambs born prematurely, plus all those who help to keep up his style of living. There are thousands of dollar millionaires in the second rank, and hundreds of thousands in the third rank. Although the latter are less privileged and therefore spend less per head, they still as a group waste a good deal more and create a good deal more pollution than Versailles ever did in the seventeenth century, because there are so many of them.

Then finally there are hundreds of millions of *us,* by which I mean all those of us who take advantage of the consumer society, who have a car, or even two cars, for our leisure-hours – and this will soon include more than half the population in the developed capitalist countries (i.e. in North America, Australasia and Western Europe). Plus of course the tens of millions who constitute the privileged minorities

48

in the socialist countries and the dominated countries (i.e. the ones more often labelled 'underdeveloped').

The privileges of wealth may be fairly common (which is more accurate than to say that they are distributed on a democratic basis) – think, for instance, of the North American manual worker in Detroit with his huge car (or a child who's bought over two hundred toy cars by the age of eight). But this does not in any way justify the situation. The life-style enjoyed by such people could never spread right across the globe, firstly because there aren't enough resources to go round, and secondly because we'd all be choked to death from pollution. This would soon call into question such a life-style, if we opted for a universalist and socialist solution that would give equal priority to social justice across the globe and to survival. We'll therefore have to tackle the privileged of this world as a group, which means the majority of us, *including you and me,* by quoting some of the more blatant examples.

## 2  *Proteins for every child*

In 1971 69 million metric tons of fish were caught at sea, for 3·6 thousand million people. The tonnage is rising extremely fast, for it was under 34 million in 1958. This means that it has more than doubled in 13 years, whereas in those same 13 years agricultural output in the dominated countries barely kept up with population growth. If this fish was all intended for human consumption and was distributed on an absolutely equal basis we would have an annual per capita figure of 19 kilograms (say, 14 kilograms once the head, skin, bones etc. have been removed).

Now if priority were given to children in poor families we could easily give them twice the amount each. All of the fish is available and a high proportion, over a third, is now being turned into fish-meal, which is easy to transport anywhere in the world. If it is to be used for human consumption its quality can be improved by removing the smell, and ways of using it in cooking that seem palatable to the great majority of the populations in question have been devised.

But the problem is that those who most need the proteins

49

haven't got any purchasing power, which means that they have to go without, except for the small amounts handed out on a charitable basis. As a result virtually all the fish-meal finishes up in the feeding-troughs of our domestic animals – milch-cows, pigs and cattle bred for the slaughter-house, laying hens or chickens being fattened for market. After they've eaten it these animals turn it into milk, eggs and meat, which contain only a very small proportion of the proteins in the fish they ate.

So this is a form of wastage. It's made worse by the fact that the under-productive natural prairies and the land allowed to lie fallow to prevent it being over-cultivated could be sown with young grass, maize or field-beans, and could thus produce enough vegetable proteins to feed our breeding stocks. Some of us eat far too much meat, fish, eggs and milk (think of the Australians with their breakfast steaks), and may even be damaging our health. Now this type of wastage is increasing rapidly, since the proportion of fish that is turned into meal, almost all of which is used as animal fodder, has risen from 14 per cent in 1958 to 30 per cent in 1965 and 36 per cent in 1970. Another point: the fish used to make meal are caught too young, which is bad for the yield in subsequent years.

One solution that would combine social justice and economic rationalization would be to give the fish-meal to children in the poor countries (for instance, the children in the Andes aren't far from the fishing-grounds in Peru). After all the New Declaration of the Rights of the Child adopted by the General Assembly of the United Nations on 20 November, 1959 promised them food, housing, leisure, adequate medical care and free education.

Today, in 1973, when we can no longer hope to see this declaration put into practice throughout the world unless there is a total breakdown of the system to which even the United Nations is attached, it seems to me to be a monstrous piece of hypocrisy. We have got one organization that could handle the distribution of food, UNICEF, and it often does good work. If countries throughout the world clubbed together to give it the necessary funds a special fund for proteins could be set up. UNICEF could then draw on it to buy an increasing proportion of the fish-meal and powdered milk that is now fed to animals, and supervise its distribution. In a recent incident a farmer's wife suffocated her clerk because he had eaten some powdered milk intended for her calves!

Yet to give our surplus powdered milk to calves is the biggest wastage of all, since in a genuinely fair economy it would be restricted to the children of poor families. What is more, the amount of vegetable proteins available would be enough to give the whole of the present world population enough to eat, if only we didn't waste so much there as well. For thousands of years in China, and more recently in the United States, products based on the soya bean have been an important factor in the nation's diet. Yet virtually all the oil-cakes made from soya beans, groundnuts and coconuts are used as cattle-fodder. Now we've all nibbled roast peanuts and eaten coconut buns, which only goes to show that provided it hasn't been attacked by fungus, this cattle-cake has a very very high food value for man. Where it is now used as animal fodder it could be replaced by grass from artificial prairies.

3   *A dog in America spends more than an Indian*

According to Robert Lattés: 'In 1967, industrial production of dogfoods represented roughly the same sum per dog as the *average* income in India.' Which means a good deal more than the income of a *poor* Indian. Writing in *Le Monde* (22 August 1972), Gérard Chalencon tells us that 1 French household in 3 has a dog and at least 1 in 4 a cat, the highest figures in Europe. The consumption of petfood (or at least of food intended for pets) rose from 14 million tins in 1961 to 280 million in 1970. In all pets consume 2 million metric tons of food, or enough to give 12 million Asiatic children a decent diet, since petfood, catfood in particular, has a high protein content. I realize that it's nice to have a pet about the house, but should we put pets before children? If the world population figures were lower, if all children were well fed I shouldn't mind so much seeing pets being looked after better than Vietnamese children.

The turnover for petfood is rising by 20–25 per cent every year and has already caught up with that for baby foods! It will soon top the figure for baby foods, since 'only 1 cat in 10 and 1 dog in 7 is fed with commercially prepared foods'. Whalemeat, which will soon be unobtainable, is one ingredient in catfood and dogfood, which are sufficiently profitable to justify strident advertising campaigns. If you put the contented-looking animals on the petfood posters side by side with the photos of starving children you'd have an appropriate symbol of our civilization. In Britain the Royal Society for the Prevention of Cruelty to Animals was founded a hundred years before the National Society for the Prevention of Cruelty to Children!

A fairer distribution of purchasing power both on the international and on the national level is an essential pre-condition for a programme giving priority to the minimum needs of *all* children, including poor children. Such a programme would mean changing the whole structure of our economic system. If each person is to claim his right to obtain regular employment (by distributing the total number of useful jobs among all able-bodied people) and to a minimum share in the world's resources, we should have to reorganize the whole of our economic system on a completely different basis, by breaking away from the current mania for profit and capital 'profitability' as the first priority.

If we are to achieve this, by slow stages or by brute force, what we must do in essence is look for a way to make the transition to socialism, though I now realize, after watching what's been happening in Eastern Europe, Cuba, Chile, Tanzania and so on, that it's not going to be easy. Yet to give up the attempt would mean accepting that the appalling injustices in the world today will not only continue but will undoubtedly get worse – possibly leading in the near future to the end of any form of civilization. Before tackling the most difficult but most essential problem – the need for revolt – let's look more closely at the endless wastage that's going on all round us. It's not always deliberate of course, which is why we simply must become more fully aware of the problem as quickly as possible.

4 *The private car – that sublime folly*

Alfred Sauvy exposed the myth of the private car years ago, particularly in his book *Les Quatre roues de la fortune*,[1] where he looked at the problem mainly from the viewpoint of the developed countries. He has shown that if we had deliberately set out to find a way to jam up our towns we could scarcely have done better than to encourage everybody to own a car. On-street parking is available to all on a fraction of public land that is rarer and more precious in direct ratio to the size of the town. In 1945 Germany gave absolute priority to housing – which she sorely needed. But at that date France was embarking on a headlong rush for more cars. Parked outside the public baths in Montargis, a small town in the Paris basin, you can still see rows of huge American cars – their owners, though clearly well-off, haven't got a bathroom of their own!

In 1970 there was 1 car for every 2 people in the United States, or twice as many per head as in western Europe. Yet if you related these figures to the surface area, i.e. to the square kilometre, we in Europe have 9 times as many cars as they do. When we've caught up with the current US density of cars per head – which at the present rate will happen during the next ten years – we'll have 18 times as many per hectare! In 1971 the United States Congress lowered federal taxes on cars 'to improve the employment figures . . . if the towns had been rebuilt this would have provided an equally effective economic stimulus,' according to André Sasson. And that wouldn't have involved pollution. But the car lobby is a powerful one. Yet the Club of Rome's studies, which condemn the use of private cars, were financed by the Volkswagen and Agnelli Foundations and supervised by the vice-president of Fiat – a point worth remembering, that!

There's really no reason why in a world concerned with social justice the peasants of the deltas of India, Vietnam and China shouldn't one day be entitled – even if this is in the distant future – to the same comforts as the 'rich' in the West today. But as there are already more than 1,000 of them to the square kilometre in some rural areas, that would mean 500 cars to the square kilometre, or 5 per hectare! Plus of course cars from the large towns nearby – Shanghai or Canton, Bombay or Calcutta.

Just think a moment of the amount of space, concrete, buildings and so on needed for just one car in the United States: there's the private garage and the access to it, parking spaces at the office, at the supermarket; in front of public buildings etc. Work out the surface area of streets, roads and

motorways in terms of 1-car units; then add bridges and all
the complicated paraphernalia of intersections, with spaghetti-
type junctions in some cases; factories for making the cars;
workshops for servicing and repairing them; petrol stations
for filling them . . . and that's not all by a long chalk. If the
road network covers 1 per cent of the surface of the United
States, what proportion would it cover in countries where
the population figures are 50 times higher, if the level of
wealth were the same? But the United States has completely
abandoned any idea of social justice throughout the world.
We shall have to force them to think again.

If all these buildings etc. were placed end to end it's obvious
that if this scheme of things were adopted in Asia the splendid
ultra-intensive market gardens on the outskirts of Shanghai and
Canton, with four to seven vegetables following in rotation on
the same field every year, would all disappear beneath mounds
of concrete over a radius comparable to the 25–30 kilometres
of newly barren land round Los Angeles! Although Los
Angeles hasn't got a very high population density (40 inhabitants to the hectare, compared with 840 in Calcutta), the level
of pollution there is so high that sometimes, when the air is no
longer fit to breathe, cars are ordered to come to a standstill
for half an hour or three-quarters of an hour.

And it's only just beginning. Supersonic military aeroplanes
are highly pollutant; the supersonic bangs they make do a
good deal of damage; and the noise they make is getting
absolutely hellish. The Concorde is going to be expensive for
the ordinary French or British taxpayer, who is very unlikely
to be able to take advantage of it. It uses up three times as
much fuel per passenger, which means that it creates three
times as much pollution, not to mention the unbearable noise
it makes and the shock-waves it sets up when it breaks the
sound-barrier. It's purely a matter of prestige – and is therefore
totally out of place in the current situation; and what's more
it's liable to turn out to be ruinously expensive.

But let's go back to the type of privilege that has become
exorbitant, particularly in the light of what the Club of Rome
tells us, because it adds to social inequality and cuts back our
chances of survival a little further each day. The various
methods of transport are responsible for half the air pollution
in towns, and private cars alone create a good half of that
figure. If the steel and other materials, the engineers, technicians, factory workers and labourers who built the private

car, plus all the scarce resources and all the skills involved, had been put to a different use they could between them have equipped enough industrial plants throughout the world to cater for all the necessities of life in the developing countries.

Every car you buy, and you generally do so long before the previous one is past it (incidentally, it could have been made to last a lot longer), represents that much less steel for making ploughs for peasant communities in the tropics. Yet these ploughs are essential if they are to solve their difficulties and improve productivity by getting rid of their old equipment. Every time you make a more or less unnecessary journey ('I've got to go to my country cottage, to cut the lawn or look after the cat') – and incidentally you could just as well have gone by public transport – you might ponder the fact that you're helping to make the air on our planet unfit to breathe; you're increasing poverty in the Third World; you're wasting precious litres of black gold, which your descendants will have to go short of; and so on. The Chinese will be in a position to claim their share of scarce resources because they do not waste them, as their poverty and their concern for social justice and national independence prevent them from committing the same follies as us.

The man at the wheel, particularly if he's French, does not show the sunnier side of his nature. His position of power magnifies his arrogance, makes him doubly pretentious, extra-presumptuous. In Britain, the United States, Australia and New Zealand the pedestrian who has stepped on to a pedestrian crossing is always given priority – but not in France! As for Brazil, I was very nearly knocked down by a car when a red light was supposed to be protecting me; the only way I could save myself was by a rapid reflex action. Arrogance, thoughtlessness and drink are the three factors responsible for the great majority of accidents, far too many of which are caused simply by a lack of proper caution.

Magistrates are often too indulgent when it comes to 'accidental' murders. Often it's children from poor families, on bikes or on foot, who are the worst hit. President Johnson could state that more Americans were killed by the motor car than by 'his' war in Vietnam; (the number of Vietnamese deaths were not included in his calculations, since they clearly didn't have the same weight or the same importance for him). 16,000 French people were killed on the roads in 1971 (and the number is going up all the time) as against only 7,000 in

Britain, though the number of cars on the roads in the two countries is the same. The point is that in Britain there are speed limits, seat belts are more widely used* and people drink less.

However much people talk about car crashes and the hundreds of thousands of people wounded on the roads, the number of 'road' victims (oddly enough they are actually blamed on the 'deadly' roads!) is on the increase. In the words of Alfred Sauvy, 'We have cheerfully sacrificed to this game [that of giving priority to the motor car] housing, education, the telephones, town-planning, scientific research, cultural activities, even public health', and those are only the main victims. I'm sure that M. Sauvy will allow me to add to his list those who hardly rate a mention – the countless indirect victims of the motor car in the dominated countries, where the privileged few sacrifice the country's development potential to acquire luxury cars. And to think we were the ones who taught them to do so . . . .

5 *The waste of paper, plastics and non-returnable packaging*

Every winter my father used to buy 100 kilograms of granulated sugar (the idea of refining sugar is quite pointless) from the sugar-mill at Escaudoeuvres near Cambrai. He bought it in a single bag made of Bengal jute, which itself weighed 1 kilogram. Today the waiter in a café hands me one lump of sugar wrapped in paper, which often weighs as little as 5 grams. Which means 200 pieces of wrapping paper per kilogram, or 20,000 per 100 kilograms! Plus the machines for wrapping them and the time wasted in unwrapping them. Perhaps it's more hygienic? I don't believe it, considering all the dust that we're breathing in anyway. For many years now I've been buying tablets of a medicine that is completely tasteless, a mineral salt that is easy to swallow and not in the

* A law enforcing the wearing of seat belts outside built-up areas came into force in France in September 1973 (*translator's note*).

least bitter. But now all I can get is pills of the same make, in three separate wrappers. Needless to say they're more expensive, and to add insult to injury I have to waste my time unwrapping them. The pharmaceutical industry really has done well out of the National Health.

In the old days everybody used to take back their beer bottles, wine bottles, mineral water and squash bottles and so on, since you got something back on them. But as it now costs three times as much (20 centimes in France) to wash and return bottles as to use non-returnable plastic ones (7 centimes), the plastic ones are increasingly taking over. Even the small glass bottles used for beer are said to be a waste of packaging. All this adds to the mountains of rubbish we are already producing – and we've no idea what to do with it once we've filled all the quarries and marshes with refuse. So we burn it, but when plastic is burnt in the special factories that are springing up all over the place it gives off hydrochloric acid. We managed perfectly well before all the shopkeepers started handing out those endless little plastic bags. It has been forecast that 700,000 metric tons of PVC packaging will be in production in France by 1975.

The Sunday papers in New York and in many other towns from Canada to Australia are getting heavier and heavier. Every Sunday edition of the *New York Times* uses up 15–20 hectares of forest in Canada (the figure for an ordinary edition is 6 hectares). As the trees are cut close to the ground and on the whole there's no attempt at replanting, the new growth is poor. Ninety per cent of the paper is taken up with advertising, which encourages readers to waste even more on the articles advertised, many of which are far from essential. When the price of newsprint is subsidized by the State, as it is in France, this is sheer lunacy. The French newspapers *La Croix* and *Combat* claim that there should be subsidies only for the paper used to transmit information – a valid claim, I feel.

When I studied the work being done in Mali on teaching reading and writing by the new functional methods I saw what a large proportion of the meagre funds allocated to the project by UNESCO and the local government had to go on paper. On the other hand all those bits of paper that are always being thrust into our hands by force, or fixed to our car windscreens or stuffed through our letter-boxes or into our post soon add to the piles of rubbish, increasing both the volume of rubbish and the cost of removing it. I've had to throw out my ordinary wastepaper basket and use instead one of those big baskets people carry on their backs in Cambodia. And it's full virtually every day. Advertising executives and propaganda-mongers of the world, hear my plea! Even if I happened to feel like reading what you've got to say, I get so much that I wouldn't have time to read it all, even supposing I had nothing better to do with my time! On the other hand, the most basic needs of schoolchildren in Africa or Asia are not properly met. And those who've learnt to read in a vernacular that is not widely spoken cannot later find any books, brochures or newspapers in their language that are likely to interest them. So they are forced to sink back into their former illiteracy.

### 6 The misuse of advertising, which encourages waste

Advertising could perform a useful service as a channel of information if it were controlled by the consumer organizations. But Europe hasn't got her own Ralph Nader. At the moment advertising is controlled by the manufacturers, and is thus the tool of unbridled growth. It doesn't seem to me to give a very optimistic picture of human nature. Judging by the incentives generally used by the advertising man, virtually the only things that make any impression on us are sex, pride, vanity, the urge to seem, indeed to *be*, 'genuine', and to appear rich – plus greed. The advertisers are only too ready to think of us as idiots, and that's what irritates me most every time I see some special gift offer – anyone would think the manufacturer who's so eager to offer us his product was really a philanthropist at heart!

France's internal airline, Air-Inter, sends out circulars with the words 'Your air ticket is enclosed' printed on the envelope! And in France the Loterie Nationale and the state-run betting organization – which incidentally are really a tax on the poor, though they are extremely popular because they offer a glimmer of hope whenever the prospect of an afterlife seems to grow dim – also go in for a huge amount of advertising. If you want to listen to the radio news in France you've got a choice between the state-run ORTF, which is full of government propaganda, and the fringe stations, which are full of advertising. All the various stations hunt out items of news that will be popular with the mass audience – Arthur Conte* even claimed that his aim was to 'entertain' us – instead of concentrating on informing us, on turning us into the 'new man' who is so badly needed if we are to create a fairer society that is capable of survival.

Advertising is one of the pillars, one of the bases of our profit economy. If this profit economy is to prosper, or even simply to keep going, there will have to be a steady increase in consumer spending for an indefinite period of time. In the rich countries the basic needs of the most affluent sectors of society – food, housing, education, health – are more or less taken care of. But once they've paid for these basic necessities many of them still have a considerable purchasing power. So the advertisers decide to give them an incentive to spend their surplus income, generally on items they don't need. The point is that this business of squandering money has become an essential function, an indispensable driving force behind our profit economy – which is itself beginning to look increasingly irrational in the light of recent studies. Advertising is far more successful at raising people's aspirations than production, and makes virtually all of us feel unsatisfied and therefore alienated, however high our standard of living. If our 'needs' are unlimited, how on earth shall we ever arrive at the stage of communism in which everyone's needs should be fulfilled comfortably.

Fashion is a typical example. All women must automatically feel all wrong in last year's skirts, dresses and coats. Even if they've got skinny thighs or huge great thighs they feel virtually compelled to display them from time to time. Even women who look more attractive in long dresses (which is what they were urged to buy last year), because they suit their figure better, are soon being recommended to go back to the miniskirt, which has come back into its own after the very short interregnum of the long skirt – which itself lasted just long enough to encourage them to throw away their miniskirts.

* Arthur Conte, former head of French Television, whose dismissal in autumn 1973 created a great stir and gave new ammunition to those who claim that the communications media in France should be given greater freedom (*translator's note*).

Meanwhile the majority of the pretty girls in the tropics can't afford to dress properly at all – unless they resort to various forms of prostitution. When I was in Venezuela I had to fill in my neighbour's police entry form for her because although she was very smartly dressed she couldn't read or write. American businessmen tell us (*Les Informations*, 16 October, 1972) that advertising is too expensive, since it costs 20 thousand million dollars a year; that it irritates the ordinary man in the street and insults his intelligence, gives a false picture of the product concerned and is a bad influence on children . . . . Yet the advertisers have a firm hold over the newspapers, which couldn't survive without them. This means that they can steer the editorial matter in whatever direction they want, and thus distort it.

Fashion isn't restricted to clothes. It also aims to make furnishings and interior decoration seem out of date in the shortest possible time. And this is even truer of that notorious symbol of our consumer society, the motor car. Quite apart from being a questionable means of transport, the motor car is a status symbol. Too bad if there's a serious shortage of nickel, this new version of the Apple of Temptation must be with us, in all its splendour.

It's only logical for the advertisers to pull out all the stops to encourage us to throw away most of our purchases soon after we've bought them and start again. The best way to get us to do this is to make articles that are less hard-wearing and therefore don't last as long. I'm told that some groups of furniture manufacturers are giving serious thought to this problem. Jacques Duboin recalled that in about 1900 he was using mechanical razor-blades that were more or less ever-lasting. And the quality of nylon and electric light-bulbs has *deliberately* been lowered.

7 *The dead-end created by excessive urban development*

The word 'town' will no longer do for those huge urban complexes that by roughly the end of the century are going to cover virtually the whole of the Netherlands, or so the forecasters say, except for a few forests, some greenhouses and a few scattered meadows stuffed to the gills with nitrates. If the same thing happened in Sao Paulo its population – which was 9 million in 1972 and is expected to be 20 million in 1984 – could rise to over 30 million, with 200 million in the whole of Brazil, twice the 1972 figure. Tokyo and Yokohama would have met by that time. Even in 1968 I spent ages getting through the suburbs of Tokyo to the rice-fields in the country-side proper. The area between Boston and Washington will be virtually one continuous built-up area, and the same goes for the area between Paris and Rouen. The geographers have even had to dream up a specific term for these urban con-glomerations, which are contemporary with the financial conglomerates. They call them 'conurbations' or 'megalo-polises'.

No one would deny that towns have had a civilizing effect, in that they allowed men to shake off the yoke of servile labour in the fields, gave them an opportunity to think about the world around them, to work out the scientific laws underlying it, to think about the human condition, about the social and political system, and so on. Craftsmen working in towns could perfect their techniques, which had originally been designed to serve the needs of the Church, which had its own part to play in production. Urban merchants and traders evolved the system of barter. Long after the days of Master Kong (551–479[?] BC) – better known as Confucius – Socrates, Plato and Aristotle had enough time to spare – as indeed he had – to meditate on the development of our societies . . . .

The industrial revolution that occurred in the eighteenth century made it necessary for the manufacturing process to be concentrated in larger workshops and factories, so that the new sources of energy could be maximized. In the era of automation and electronics the industrialist who sets up business in Greater Paris is much more likely to be able to take on all the wide variety of labour he needs, some of which must be very highly skilled, than if he were in the provinces. And he has *the* national market on his doorstep, not simply because of the size of the population in Paris but because the average purchasing power is higher than elsewhere. His engineers' children will be able to go to what are generally thought to be the best universities and training colleges. Not to mention the allegedly better leisure facilities etc.

61

But if we examine the situation rather more closely we can see that these advantages are getting more and more expensive for a large and growing sector of the community. The working day in the factories has been cut from 14 hours in 1840 to 8 hours, but part of this gain has been offset by the longer periods of time spent travelling by public transport, which often involves upwards of 2, or sometimes 3, hours a day. I've seen Japanese women employees strap-hanging in the underground or suburban trains during the rush hour, visibly worn out because they've fallen victim to the Great God Growth. And we're told that the majority of Japanese people still refuse to take a holiday.[2]

'Suburbanization' or 'conurbation' is leading us straight to a dead-end. And the situation is made even more tragic by the fact that it is linked to the exorbitant privileges granted to the private car. The rich move out from the town centres, where the air is no longer fit to breathe; in London, for instance, the business quarter, the City, was the first area to be deserted at night. The suburbs are growing out of all proportion, and it wouldn't be difficult to work out the exact date when Western Europe would be completely covered with towns, suburbs and second homes if the towns continue to spread at the present rate. As we've said, the Netherlands will have got there by the beginning of next century, with 28 per cent of the country given over to motorways.

If the most densely populated areas in the deltas of Asia wasted land to the same extent they wouldn't have anything left to grow crops on. After all, they've already got a larger population than the figure forecast for Holland in the year 2010 – and my younger readers will still be alive then. According to the Ehrlichs,[3] every time California's population goes up by 1,000 it swallows up 96 hectares of arable land by covering it with concrete.

But Western Europe is 18 times more densely populated than the United States. And a large number of rural areas, from southern China to North Vietnam, from Bengal to Egypt and Java, already have over 1,000 people to the square kilometre, or to the 100 hectares. No doubt it was these people Rostow had in mind when he suggested that the famous 'American way of life' would be achieved by the twenty-first century (by which time they may well have twice the number of people). A more sensible estimate says that the so-called 'economies of scale' achieved by huge urban

62

complexes start becoming negative as soon as they reach a population figure of 100,000.

The level of physical pollution is becoming unbearable, particularly on still days. In some parts of New York some of the rubbish can't be carted away, and there's so much unemployment in Harlem that life is becoming impossible. All this encourages a criminal element that is no longer interested solely in money (as in Italy) now that life has been thrown further and further off balance (junkies, etc.). How many secretaries and other employees at the United Nations long for the headquarters to be moved out to a town that is genuinely more 'hospitable' than New York, the 'metropolis' of trade, industry and even intellectual life, which is virtually unlivable-in nowadays? How many of them ask to be moved to some other international organization in Geneva, Rome or Paris?

One point that has not been given sufficient emphasis up to now is the way towns act as a sort of whirlpool, sucking in and squandering all the resources that are becoming scarce. Whereas a country cottage can be made of stone, wood or earth mixed with a little cement to make it firmer (and cement's in plentiful supply), skyscrapers swallow up huge quantities of metal – which will all have been used up by the twenty-first century, if things go on as they are. The furniture and fittings used in them, their 'modern' kitchens, their electric appliances, their air-conditioning units and so on will soon use up the semi-precious metals, along with the pipes and cables for water, gas, electricity, the telephone, the sewage system etc.

Another expensive item is roads and motorways, and communications in general. As we've never managed to lay out our big towns on a logical pattern so that everyone could reach his place of work on foot or by bicycle, the fuel wasted on transport and in traffic jams also represents one of the chief sources of pollution. Claude Julien[4] tells us that the motor-buses in Paris travelled at the same speed in 1970 as the horse-drawn omnibuses did in 1890. He stresses the fact that the State has to shoulder the growing deficit of the RATP, the Paris transport organization, and 'injects new funds into the urban areas, not with the aim of making them pleasanter to live in and more profitable but instead to allow them to spread even more quickly – whereas this suburban sprawl is the root cause of the deficit'.

Whereas the British want to free London from congestion and build their new towns somewhere between 50 and 130 kilometres from the capital the French are building them only 20 or 30 kilometres away from Paris. This will result in a level of congestion that is increasingly unbearable to live in. All this seems quite idiotic, but it is easily explained by the soaring profits made by the property companies. Yet only some of the more glaring aspects of their activities are described as scandalous. It's easier to buy a piece of farm-land and pull strings to get planning permission to build on it than to rope in immigrant labour and slave-drive them into cultivating the land for you. Which explains where a sizable proportion of today's capital gains come from – after all it's not just the manufacturer who makes them.

This means that in the near future zero population growth, which, as we've already seen, is a matter of much greater urgency in the rich countries, should go hand in hand with a series of measures to slow down the scandalous spread of urban building. Unlimited urbanization is seriously damaging the environment, creating an appalling level of pollution and alienating a growing number of ordinary working people, including white-collar workers. Most of all, it is squandering resources that will very soon be unobtainable, not to mention the nervous energy that is expended when people get irritable over trifles. For many centuries Paris was a thoroughly delightful city and a walk along the banks of the Seine was a unique experience. But then Georges Pompidou decided that Paris was to be 'adapted to modern living', and agreed that the motorway on the Left Bank could go straight past Notre-Dame.

If only the drivers who roar past the cathedral would instead go inside, go down on their knees and pray that those who are responsible for our future will eventually see the light and realize that the only way to make large towns livable-in nowadays is to ban private cars from the centre, as in Berne or Geneva. The arms race, the private car and the monster-town are the chief enemies of the late twentieth century, the prime source of the wasteful habits of the privileged minorities, which are aggravating the damage done by the population explosion and uncontrolled industrial growth. But how can we make the privileged few listen to reason, as long as they've got all the power machinery tightly clasped in their hot little hands? We're going to have to give them a smart rap over the knuckles.

8 *Uncontrolled growth: do we 'need' arms – or a revolt?*

There's no point now in making do with criticizing this or that millionaire, this or that pressure group, sugar lobby or even the whole military and industrial complex. The economic system of the capitalist countries is caught up in a movement that is more or less irreversible as long as it stays the same, as long as imperialism prevails, as long as dominance of all kinds persists, as long as the Great God Profit holds sway. If France is to keep her balance of payments favourable she must sell arms to her foreign clients. So she makes up to South Africa and strengthens the policy of apartheid, in defiance of the straightforward respect for dignity felt by the Africans. She sells more and more arms to the non-developed countries, realizing that in so doing she is jeopardizing their future development. After all she must 'keep her balance of payments favourable' – if only so as to be able to stock up with oil, ores, luxury foods and so on, thus allowing her privileged minority to squander at will.

The economic system of the capitalist countries has admittedly proved capable of adapting itself to a certain extent. It now accepts state intervention, which was so abhorrent to the United States right up to 1930, when the virtual lack of it helped to worsen the Great Depression. The system actually requires the State to step in now whenever this would be advantageous, in the form of subsidies, credits from state-run banks, 'protective' tariffs and so on. But the economic experts do not seem at all inclined to bring about the full-scale revolution – for this time a mere change of direction is no longer enough – that the Club of Rome feels to be essential. Yet the members of the Club of Rome have not been sufficiently specific in their recommendations. What we need this time is for the influential people to commit suicide, to perform an act of hara-kiri, precisely because they are influential. Now it's difficult enough to give up your share of the profits, but even more difficult to give up the attributes

65

of influence and power – which, as we all know, corrupts.

More and more of us are beginning to accept the values of socialism, particularly, according to Yves Goussault, the younger generation. But this doesn't answer the problem of how we're going to get there. The most enlightened people in the rich world, and even some of those responsible for running the monthly review *L'Esprit,* can't manage to think things out properly because they don't take fully into account the extreme poverty in the under-developed countries. For the simple reason that they can't really take it in unless they've observed it over a long period. They're still too caught up with the minutiae of internal French politics. And as for the young people who have grasped the extreme seriousness of the situation better than anyone by subjecting it to a very subtle analysis, I'm told by a girl I know that only too often they take refuge in a 'gather-ye-rosebuds' attitude. The idea of 'Après nous le déluge' didn't by any means end with the eighteenth century. It is only too readily adopted by many irresponsible people, who are nothing short of drop-outs.

In Part IV I shall be putting forward my conclusions about the diet of semi-austerity that we shall have to accept if we are to bring the sufferings of the under-privileged to an end. But it's already only too plain that the great majority of ordinary working people in the rich countries, and their representatives, aren't going to like them one bit. As soon as you add to the list the private car run by the ordinary working-class family you're likely to see your popularity dwindle at the next elections . . . .

The Hungarian Marxist Georg Lukacs, an extremely clever man (which was enough to make some people suspect him of heresy), has already spoken out against a common error committed by the various Communist Parties, who tend to sacrifice their long-term strategy on the altar of mere tactics, of short-term profits. Patrick Chaussepied has recently come back from East Germany, where people are turning out to be 'Cartierist' in their fashion.* They put it like this: 'If we weren't lumbered with those incompetent Rumanians and Bulgarians our standard of living would go up much more

* The term *cartiérisme* has recently been coined to describe the type of views held by one of France's best-known journalists and broadcasters, Raymond Cartier, joint managing director of *Paris-Match,* who argues that far too much financial aid is being given to the Third World (*translator's note*).

quickly.' In spite of a huge propaganda campaign the people of pre-1968 Czechoslovakia showed little enthusiasm for stepping up their 'aid' to the Third World. Admittedly they had plenty of other arguments to bring up against their then government.

There seems to be little point in hoping, as J.-F. Revel* does, that a full-scale revolution will blow up tomorrow in the United States. The various protest movements there are highly likely to remain minority movements in spite of the interesting fact that some of them – not all – reject the consumer society. Others, on the other hand, particularly the poorest elements, are hoping for a larger slice of the consumer cake. The working class in all the rich countries is in an ambiguous position, though it doesn't like admitting it. It's quite willing to claim that it's being exploited, which it is. But it won't admit that it may also be exploiting the dominated countries in certain ways.

As we in France saw over the weekend of 1 June, 1968,† the mere fact of possessing a private car is undeniably a step on the road to *embourgeoisement* – and *le weekend* has become too sacrosanct to be sacrificed to a demonstration, even if this might turn out to be the beginning of the Revolution. The spread of the private car is paving the way for a generation of selfish people who will be moving further and further away from the 'new man' whom Che Guevara so longed for. And yet the society of tomorrow will desperately need this 'new man'. According to the 4 October, 1972 issue of the French communist daily *L'Humanité*, 'There is no justification for restricting consumption among ordinary people.' Admittedly the first step will be to cut back the consumption of the rich. But on the global scale anyone who has a private car which he can use for leisure-time activities is exorbitantly rich, an exploiter.

Marx told us in essence that the interests of the most exploited classes were the same as those of the whole of

* Jean-François Revel, literary and political editor of the influential French weekly *L'Express* (*translator's note*).
† During the disturbances in May 1968 petrol was unobtainable in France for several weeks. After General de Gaulle's speech at the end of the month and the big pro-government demonstration in the Champs-Elysées the filling stations were suddenly able to get supplies again. As a result, instead of 'continuing the fight' the vast majority of Parisians took to their cars for their first outing for weeks and the anti-Gaullist demonstrations fizzled out (*translator's note*).

mankind. This still appears to be the case, provided that we now look for these 'most exploited people' outside our consumer society, outside the sector of working-class people who have risen to join the ranks of the middle classes – and they are now in the majority in the rich countries – and the other working people in the rich countries. These 'most exploited' people are chiefly to be found in the dominated countries, once we've discounted the privileged minorities in such countries. This means that we must once again take a quick look at the so-called 'developing countries', as though we were visiting them as foreign observers.

The multinational companies and the giants that have emerged as a result of mergers are busy diversifying their activities and are cornering an increasingly large share of economic power. In spite of a number of attempts by people like General de Gaulle to shake them off, they have on the whole managed to get their hands on the major political decisions made in the rich countries, which are often lumped together – somewhat hastily – under the single heading 'Imperialism'. As the majority of people in the rich countries have access to certain privileges of a kind that can never, as we now know, be available to everyone on a global basis, there's no point in counting on them to abandon these privileges voluntarily. The night of 4 August 1789* is easier to explain if you remember that it was preceded by a whole lot of mansions and castles being set on fire . . . .

You might perhaps say that, with the Palestinians at the Munich Olympic Games, on the global level we have now reached the year 1780. As with the third estate, the Third World has little hope left if the present political and economic system continues, since it is highly likely that it will condemn the majority of the world's population to poverty in perpetuity, by spreading its tentacles to dominate more and more people. Up to now I've always refrained from recommending our young friends in the dominated countries to take up any specific form of direct action, even when they asked for my views. I felt that a decision of this kind was so important, would bring about so many difficult and unforeseeable results, that it must be left to those directly concerned.

* After bands of peasants had roamed the countryside burning down their châteaux the nobility renounced their feudal privileges during the 4 August, 1789 session of the new Assemblée Nationale Constituante, which had been set up by all three estates on 9 July (*translator's note*).

But the risks involved now seem to me so appalling that I am duty bound to offer them a solemn warning. That's what I am aiming to do in this book, though of course it will be read only by the privileged few. The time has now come to look more closely into the implications of these new concepts for the future of the dominated countries – a future that they clearly won't accept if the picture is too black. At the UNCTAD* congress held in Santiago in April and May 1972 the dominated countries presented the document framed by the Lima Declaration of October 1971 (they had met in time to prepare for the Santiago congress). They stated that since the Geneva congress in 1964 no progress whatsoever had been made on a joint basis on helping their products to reach the markets in the developed countries. They called for an end to tariff barriers and internal taxes; or, while this was being organized, for their produce to be transferred to the other dominated countries. Their next stipulation was that a fixed percentage of the consumption of each product should be allocated to imports from the developing countries. Finally, remunerative, fair and stable prices should be obtained for products from the developing countries, so as to maintain and increase the purchasing power of exported products in relation to essential imports.

In its *Report and Prospects for Produce* 1971–2 the FAO offers a résumé of the work done at this congress, on which I based the passage above, and adds: 'These proposals were not accepted by the developed countries with a market economy, who submitted their own resolution . . . . The conference decided to send these two plans to its permanent machinery . . .', which is a way of burying them, or at any rate postponing them. M. Giscard d'Estaing had admittedly made a very generous speech at the opening session . . . .

And now he is calling for a levelling out of inequalities in France – providing we put our trust in a majority party that has continually helped to increase the very same inequalities over the last 15 years – particularly on the global level.

* United Nations Conference on Trade and Development.

Part III

# REVOLTS ARE INEVITABLE IN THE DOMINATED COUNTRIES

1    *There've been plenty of warnings*

Let's make the point yet again: the hopes raised by development – itself a formula that is sufficiently vague to retain a touch of the miraculous – are being shattered one after the other. The dominated countries are running up debts at breakneck speed. You'd have to be pretty naive nowadays – or at any rate pretend to be – to go on believing that the 80 thousand million dollars they 'owed' in 1973 will ever be repaid. The debts incurred by the Russians after 1917 have never been 'honoured', nor have China's after 1949, and the same goes for many other foreign loans. Why should the Third World's debts be repaid when the United States refuses to give up her overseas interests to repay her own debts (particularly those with the issuing banks), which have now become irrecoverable as well, since the 'crash' of 15 August, 1971?

There's been a series of congresses on Trade and Development, from Geneva in 1964 to New Delhi in 1968 and Santiago in 1972, but of course they all fail for the same reason – the rich nations won't give way. In 1969 Lester Pearson made a fine-sounding report to the World Bank, the essence of which was to advise the rich nations to 'be nicer' (which is what the churches advised and are still advising)! And the rich nations do sometimes reach into their pockets and hand over a few coppers if they think this will help their own situation, as McNamara explains, by helping to bolster up a system that they do well out of, even if they don't recover all their debts. The United Nations has organized a second 'decade of development' for the seventies and there were hopes that it would be more successful than the previous decade, the sixties, but it's already getting bogged down. According to G. Viratelle (*Le Monde*, 25 November, 1972) the industrial growth rate in India was as high as 8 per cent in 1955–66 but fell to 3.7 per cent in 1970–1.

Yet on 15 August, 1971 Mr Nixon axed all the fine-sounding projects for aid included in these recommendations, sweeping them aside in favour of giving priority to 'the defence of the dollar'. Aid has been cut back still further and the protective duties have increased – the poor nations must just get along as best they can! It's difficult to envisage the extent to which the most elementary principles of social justice are being mocked – though admittedly if the idea of demolishing Vietnam piece by piece is accepted as permissible anything else seems perfectly legitimate.

Yet there's no shortage of people to point out the dangers. Arghiri Emmanuel has told us that any form of trade between countries with unequal powers must inevitably be unequal. Gunder Frank thinks that what we have is a situation where *under*-development is itself developing, particularly in Latin America. Samir Amin has shown how the world's money has been concentrated at the 'headquarters' of the worldwide capitalist system, i.e. in the developed countries, rather than on the outskirts, i.e. in the dominated countries. Pierre Jalée has taken apart the machinery by which the Third World is being stripped of its resources; Paul Bairoch has described the Third World as being 'at a dead end'; and Tibor Mende heralds a logical progression from aid to recolonization.[1] A large number of other studies along the same lines could be mentioned here.

A whiff of anxiety is at last being felt in United Nations circles, possibly because the personal circumstances of the 'experts' who take part in the discussions are pretty enviable. The UN Committee for Development Planning, which up to now has been chiefly concerned with 'growth' expressed solely in terms of GNP, is at last (after being told to do so over and over again for years) beginning to notice that:

> ... unemployment and mass poverty, instead of being contained, are actually on the rise in many developing countries. Worse, the report says, government policies of accelerated development may in some cases unwittingly aggravate the problem....
> ... The number of jobs new industries have created has been

small, and the prosperity they have spread *has gone into the hands of a relative few* . . . .

. . . By rigid adherence to a highly structured educational system, copied from the West, many developing countries have merely produced large numbers of educated unemployed . . . .

'Employment and mass poverty,' says the committee, 'must be moved from the periphery to the centre of all development planning.' [2]

## 2 *Over-urbanization and growing unemployment among young people*

Who runs the 'planning bodies'? Both in the dominated countries and in the developed countries the reins of power are held by the privileged minority, whose 'dominating' concern is not under-employment or poverty but a more general instinct to keep themselves in power by any means available to them, even if it means going against the wishes of the electorate. I was absolutely flabbergasted to hear the French President singing the praises of neo-colonialism in Fort-Lamy, where the French army was helping to keep an unpopular government in power by force.*

Westernized methods of education encourage the sons of tropical peasants to look with longing at the jobs of civil servants, who are themselves in a privileged position. The privileges enjoyed by civil servants are ruinously expensive for the economic system in the poor countries, since an excessive proportion of the GNP is syphoned off to maintain bureaucrats who often have little concern for the national interest and whose consumption of luxury goods, imported at great expense, is far too high. As a result the possibilities for modernization in agriculture and industry in such countries are being jeopardized.

An even greater threat is posed by the resultant disenchant-

* In 1971 the French Government sent a task-force of the Foreign Legion to combat the activities of anti-government rebels in the republic of Chad in Central Africa, at the request of the Chad government and in accordance with the co-operation agreement between the two countries (*translator's note*).

73

ment with agriculture and life on the land. Except in a few rare instances, anyone who stays in his peasant community – which, as I've shown, is often on its last legs – has no hope of improving his social standing. So a young man with a rudimentary education will set off for the nearest big town to look for a job in the tertiary sector, which soon becomes overcrowded, to the detriment of general production and public amenities such as hospitals, schools, roads and so on. In a study of urban unemployment in the developing countries Paul Bairoch[3] has shown that between 1950 and 1970 the number of people out of work in the towns in the developing countries taken together (and his figures have been worked out very carefully) may well have risen from 7 million to 22 million, or from 2 to 3.5 per cent of the whole working population. But if we take the figures for the *urban* working population alone there was a rise from 10 to 12 per cent. Most significant of all, the level of unemployment among young people between 15 and 24 is more than twice that of the population as a whole.

In working out his figures for the 15–24 age-group Bairoch notes that 39 per cent are unemployed in the towns in Ceylon, 40 per cent in Guyana, 26 per cent in Trinidad and Tobago and so on, which proves that dominated economic systems of this kind are increasingly unable to find their young people jobs in the productive industries. The highest rate of unemployment is among young people who have attended school for between 6 and 11 years – which is an appalling indication of failure both for the type of education given and for the economic system in the dominated countries. To these figures we must also add an enormous level of *under*-employment, which corresponds to an excessive growth in the tertiary sector, given the stage of development reached by the various countries.

According to Bairoch, 'In 1960 the proportion of people employed in the tertiary sector in southern and eastern Asia was very similar to the figure for Europe in 1850, whereas their revenue was of the order of 50 per cent below Europe at that period.' He believes that over-employment in the urban sector is initially the result of 'a mass influx of people of working-age who have been cast out by the rural community'. It is therefore tied up with the shortage of jobs in rural areas. This leads to a drop in agricultural output, which in turn slows down the whole process of development, mainly as a result of the need to import more food. And yet the poor are starving in Bangladesh.


### 3 The difficulties involved in modernizing agriculture; the situation in Niger

The first aim of us rich countries was to develop production in the dominated countries of goods that we wanted ourselves and for which we opened up a market. The great discoveries tended to take away the Arab merchants' monopoly in spices such as cinnamon, cloves or pepper, or at any rate this was the eventual result. Then we planted sugar-cane in Brazil and the Antilles, tobacco and cotton in the southern United States, coffee in Santo Domingo and Brazil, and so on. At the end of the nineteenth century huge rubber and palm-tree plantations were developed in Malaysia and Indonesia, and then spread in the twentieth century to Indochina and Africa. In the nineteenth century tea, which originated in China, began to cover the hillsides and mountainsides of Assam and later Ceylon, in the form of huge 'European' plantations; and now it's being planted in eastern Africa as well . . . .

At the same time colonization by the European countries was ruining trades that were more highly developed than our own, such as that of textile-workers in India and China; craftsmen who had been robbed of their daily bread by our mechanized industries were sent back to the land, which was itself already overcrowded. Throughout this period of development, the production of food crops was held back by exports, and the potential of the home market, which had already been cut back by the general spread of poverty, could not be fully exploited. From 1896 to 1900, when famine was raging throughout the Indian Empire, British ships were calmly being loaded in Karachi with cargoes of wheat – which the starving Indians naturally couldn't afford. The same goes for a sizable proportion of the rice crop in Indochina, which was being force-fed to our livestock while the local people, particularly from 1930 to 1939, often had none for themselves. During this period, the 'Tonkinese' were reduced to eating sweet potatoes.

75

It is generally claimed that since the dominated countries were 'liberated' things have greatly improved and the local peasantry is being properly looked after. Yet the first thing the French did between 1942 and 1946 was to set up a series of specialized institutes (which incidentally have done some good work) to deal solely with crops grown for export (oil seeds, textiles, bananas and pineapples, coffee and cocoa, rubber). It wasn't until 1960 that any proper attempt was made to promote the cultivation of food-crops and stock-breeding. And then again such attempts were often not properly directed. I have listed many examples of this in my earlier books, along with many other authors.

Ninety-three per cent of the population in Niger still lives on the land, and virtually all of them are engaged in crop-growing or stock-breeding. Since independence, which was granted in the early sixties, the emphasis has been on irrigation, which is a very expensive business in this area; the French experts who were consulted generally recommended this policy. Now before they can grow crops successfully under irrigation the local peasantry must have acquired a high level of technical skill and must have been, as it were, forced to go in for intensive farming because they are short of land. A peasant class of this kind exists in the Far East, but not in tropical Africa. The cost of this kind of development, which is not very high by Asian standards, is essentially taken care of in China by human investment. The Chinese peasant often invests 50–100 days per annum of unpaid labour in the land. In Tatchai the figure is 112-plus!

The equipment used in Niger has been paid for by overseas funds, which means that the country is even more financially – and politically – dependent. But most of the running costs have to come out of the national exchequer, and they soon become ruinous. When we turn to output figures we see that whereas the technicians of Formosa harvest 12 metric tons of paddy to the hectare, growing two crops a year on their trial fields, even the most efficient Nigerian peasants can't manage more than 7 metric tons. As a result, since 1971 priority has been given to intensifying traditional methods of dry-farming, which can be developed more rapidly and more economically than irrigation.

Meanwhile over a period of 11 years the major portion of the resources of a very poor country have been spent on ruinously expensive equipment. During these same 11 years, there has been no attempt to control the population, which has risen from 3 million to 4 million; and the current annual growth rate has been estimated at 2.7 per cent, with agricultural output nowhere near keeping up. This population explosion represents the main obstacle in the path of development. It's alarming to think that in a country where it's turning out to be very difficult to step up agricultural output, thanks to unfavourable natural conditions, the usual forecast is that the population will have topped 8 million before the century is out! In Niamey the population is increasing by 10 per cent per annum, and Jean Ruche states: 'This movement is robbing the countryside of a young and active sector of the population and is cluttering up the capital with huge numbers of unemployed people who cannot be absorbed into a secondary sector that has seen little development so far, or into a disproportionately large tertiary sector.'[4] Now that the system of letting land lie fallow has been abandoned the effects of droughts are becoming even more serious (1972).

#### 4   Will dominance and poverty ever end?

If the present rate of progress continues the future prospects for the dominated countries look very dim. The gulf between rich and poor would not only continue to exist, it would also continue to widen. Jean Ruche wonders whether it will ever be possible even to maintain the present standard of living in Niger, let alone raise it. In northern Senegal food shortages are causing increasing hardship. In the semi-arid regions of East Africa famine rages during the dry years, as it does in the Nordeste region of Brazil and over a large part of the Indian subcontinent. Meanwhile the privileged few are planning to take it easy, which means that they'll waste a bit more and pollute a bit more every year. If there's one thing I'm certain of, it's that injustice on this scale can't go on much longer.

According to the forecasts worked out by the Club of Rome, the majority of people in the dominated countries are in great danger of being condemned to poverty in perpetuity if today's economic structures are left as they are. Factors such as the worsening of terms of trade, continuing unequal trading, the growing difficulty in amassing capital, the maintenance of economic dominance by multinational companies, and of neo-imperialist political dominance by the rich nations, are leading them down a whole series of blind-alleys.

A different development policy is already in operation in the most densely populated country in the world – China. The Chinese system does certainly allow for a moderate level of growth, but this is achieved without overseas aid, without unemployment, without waste and with very little pollution. It's true of course that factors such as natural conditions, historical heritage, social customs, level of development and particularly recent political history vary widely from one country to another in tropical Africa, South America and southern Asia, and that all of them are very different from the situation in China.

A dogmatic carbon copy of the methods used in China could not be applied elsewhere. For instance, I can't see Tanzania's 'Ujamaa villages',* which are floundering along amid a welter of difficulties aggravated by red tape, being transformed into Chinese-style people's communes in the near future. Even the Chinese don't advise this. But a number of principles do seem to be generally valid, though the distortions created by imperialism are making it increasingly difficult to apply them. I shall now try to pick out a few of the principles that seem to me most urgent if the present trend is to be reversed and the poor countries are to be freed from dominance. As a first step I shall see genuine economic independence as the goal, though this is essentially a *political* problem.

5 *The deadlock we've reached is first and foremost a political one: 60 per cent of Indians 'are clinging on to a life of abject poverty'*

I took part in the studies conducted under the wing of the Sebou Project, which was set up to investigate the possibilities for developing the whole of the basin of the only

* A reference to Julius Nyerere's experiment in collective organization in Tanzanian villages, instigated in 1967 (*translator's note*).

78

great river in northern Morocco. The project recommended a number of agricultural structures that were better suited to making more effective use of very expensive irrigation methods, with co-operative groups providing credit facilities and services; in particular the land under irrigation should be distributed on a more equal basis. The Moroccan government would not allow the Project's report to be published, since, like any economic decision, it involved political repercussions: 'politics is at the command-post'.

In 1967 King Hassan II told me that the aim of his agricultural policy was not to stir up trouble, to keep everyone happy. I told him that I believed that the worst possible agricultural policy seemed to me preferable to no policy at all, providing you knew how to put your mistakes right, since at least you'd be moving forwards. Stagnation, the maintenance of the *status quo* ultimately represent a step backwards and are thus the worst solution of all. What he was really determined to do was to give a helping hand to the 'bigwigs' in his entourage, and to make a pile for himself – which he seems to have done. In December 1970, when some peasants took up arms to prevent a rich Moroccan from taking over some property belonging to a colonist (Menziès) – the Moroccan had friends at court, which meant that he could get round the law – the police fired, killing several people. The government, alarmed, speeded up the process of handing over to the fellaheen small parcels of land for settling, in the sectors watered by the first irrigation channels. One of my pupils worked out at the time how many peasants would have to die before the land would be distributed on an equal basis! After 16 August, 1972 the king decided on a second handout of 90,000 hectares of colonizing land, or half the amount that had been distributed over 15 years; this came to less than 181,000 hectares out of a total of 8 million hectares under cultivation in Morocco (i.e. just over 2 per cent). But this land was above average in quality and in many cases irrigated. Let's hope that more handouts will follow. Corruption is so rife that even the army, which supports the regime at vast expense and enjoys considerable privileges, has risen up twice against a government which has even sunk so low as to try to kidnap schoolgirls to appease the royal appetite.

In their book *Poverty in India* V. M. Dandekar and N. Rath stress the fact that in 1960–1 40 per cent of the rural population lived on under 15 rupees (about £1 per capita) per month.

The same level of poverty was reached in the towns with 22 rupees a month, and half the population had less than that. These figures lead P. Gavi, who quotes Dandekar and Rath in his book *Le Triangle Indien*,[5] to say that in that year 40 per cent of the rural population and 50 per cent of the urban population were living below the physiological minimum.

From 1960–1 to 1968–9 India's GNP increased by less than 3 per cent per annum, while the population rose by slightly over 2.5 per cent. The difference between the two figures is negligible and only the rich get any real advantage from it. Dandekar thus stresses that a proportion of the teeming urban population lives in absolute poverty. The *Economic Times* of Bombay thinks that the percentage of the population living below the poverty line rose from 52 per cent in 1960–1 to 70 per cent in 1967–8. And G. Viratelle tells us that in 1972 60 per cent of Indians were hanging on to life in a state of abject poverty, with less than 0.7 of a rupee (less than 4p) per day. When the United Nations sent me to study the work of 'community development' in India in 1958–9 Julia Henderson at the UN told me that the community development was a redoubtable secret weapon against communism – just look what it's led to!

In the face of evolution on this scale the 'development' that the international organizations are so fond of talking about is first and foremost too modest, considering the present population growth; secondly, it corresponds to a level of indebtedness that is rising too fast, and thus to increased economic dependence on foreign countries. It finishes up by reinforcing the position of the privileged minorities in the country in question, which are often hand in glove with foreign economic interests, as in the Ivory Coast. It cannot ever rescue the great mass of working people from their poverty, apart from a few semi-privileged people in the more modern sector of the economy.

If this widespread misery continues, or even increases, there's a danger that it will be perpetuated until the world's mineral stocks are exhausted, which would make any effective development designed to improve the lot of all working people much more difficult. There seems to be no way out of this situation for the great mass of peasant communities and young people out of work, against whom the authorities are quick to resort to violence – which justifies the violence being used against them, at this very moment, by the young rebels in Sri Lanka (Ceylon) or the Tupamaros in Uraguay, by the Naxalites in Bengal or the *Violencia* movement in Colombia, by people ranging from Mozambique and Angola to what is left of Portuguese Guinea. Not forgetting Vietnam, where the revolt against foreign domination is both socialist and nationalist in spirit.

In China civil strife lasted for many a long year and led to the Communist Party's seizing power. In his book *Le Monde Chinois* Jacques Gernet shows that in the China of 1895–1949 there were 'parasitic and widespread developments that were bound up with the introduction of foreign capital and industries into China itself and with widespread impoverishment, with the rural masses bearing the brunt of this.'[6] Doesn't that suggest quite a few points of comparison with the situation in the dominated countries today?

### 6  Revolts are inevitable – will they lead to chaos or to Utopia?

I'm not trying to set myself up as a prophet here – after all the race of the great prophets is dead and gone. But we can and must say if we think (particularly when, as now, it's a matter of urgency) that things don't look as bright as the orthodox conformism of the smug and the influential of this world would have us believe. Thus as early as 1959 I gave the facts about the agricultural defeat in India,[7] which took firm shape in 1965–6 and unfortunately is not yet over. Then in 1962 I wrote that Black Africa had got off to a false start. There was nothing particularly clever about these forecasts and I'm genuinely sorry that subsequent events have shown only too clearly that I was right; or that, say, Cuba's sugar harvest failed in 1972; or again that in 1972 the Soviet Union, with the largest amount of agricultural land in the world at her disposal – even if it isn't the best land in the world – had to buy 25 million metric tons of cereals from abroad.[8]

As an agronomist-cum-economist I feel less at home in the political arena – which is as closely linked to sociology and psychology as it is to economics – though I have already been caught up in politics, whether I liked it or not. And this in spite of the fact that I've specified that the action that must be taken cannot be decided on fairly by anyone other than those directly concerned, or at any rate by the best brains among them. Che Guevara paid dearly for the fact that the Revolution doesn't travel well. It is just about permissible for those who haven't got some magic recipe for revolution to envisage a few possible hypotheses, particularly if their aim is to put the 'haves' on their guard, since they are sometimes unaware that they *are* 'haves'.

Justified revolts could well lead to international wars that will swallow up the original initiative, even if all that happens is that today's conflicts spread (the hottest points at the moment being Vietnam and the Middle East). These wars could soon degenerate into nuclear suicide, particularly when more countries possess their own bombs. The richest countries, with their extremely complex societies and their excessive dependence on outside supplies (electricity, food transported over long distances, huge urban complexes etc.), would have a much harder job escaping from this spiral than the agrarian societies of Africa, or even the people's communes in China, which incidentally were planned partly with this in mind.

I shall now study a number of possible ways of creating a series of Utopias that are more or less workable. They will look Utopian to the rich nations in particular, and to the rich people in the poor nations, because they won't give up their privileges with a good grace. Until, that is, the day comes – and it won't be long now – when they understand that they are in danger of taking the whole planet, themselves included, to the brink of the abyss, perhaps even into the abyss. I say that these 'Utopias' are workable because some of them have already been put into practice, and others are being put into practice at this very moment, mainly in China, but also in Chile, Tanzania and Peru, and in some of the 'socialist' countries, though the majority of the latter are now at the stage of having a state-run economic system rather than being genuinely socialist.

I shall examine a number of aspects of what I shall call the potential for organized revolt. It would ultimately be in our own interest to help such revolts along if they turned out to be capable of leading to a fairer society and one that is better suited to survival than our own, in the first instance by avoiding nuclear catastrophe. Yet in order to show that the aim must be to combine daring reforms with clear-cut breaks with the past, smashing the yoke of the old political and economic structures, I have used the term 'revolt'. The idea is in essence to find a way of breaking completely – though not necessarily all at once – with an economic system based on profit that is at this very moment leading us *all* to our ruin. I'm glad to say that the time is well and truly over when generals and government leaders could hope to die in their beds while waiting to be beatified by having statues set up in public squares to honour their memory.

But I shan't be discussing the techniques to be used in these revolts, or guerrilla organization or the workings of the 'avant-garde' political parties (or of those who sometimes emerge in the rear). I'm not trying to write a manual for the Revolution, since it won't have much in common with the revolution over there, where conditions are so very different. I shall look for ways of adapting our economic system to the different stages in the process of transformation that seems to me essential. In sorting out my ideas I certainly shan't end up roughing out a revolutionary scheme that is universally valid. In essence, I shall try to examine once again some of the possible ways of making the transition to various different forms of socialism. This transition is essential because the way in which power is seized will largely determine the *type* of power that will emerge in the next phase. There's no point in setting our sights on power until we've clarified what exactly it is we hope for in the future.

7    *The first revolt: the achievement of national independence 'based on a country's own resources' and priority for agriculture*

According to this model power would already have passed into the hands of a team of people who would put their faith in a neutralist, non-aligned foreign policy. They would try to be on good terms with everybody, but would be determined to put the national interest first and to defend it against any attempt at dominance from abroad, while at the same time preventing the privileged minorities at home from taking

83

unfair advantage of their position. Let's give an example of this kind of situation: Tanzania since 6 February, 1967 (the date of the Arusha Declaration), under the leadership of Julius Nyerere, with whom the leaders of former French colonies such as Léopold Senghor of Senegal or Félix Houphouët-Boigny of the Ivory Coast can scarcely compare.

According to this model, the 'pro-Independence' authorities might attempt first of all to 'control the heights of the economy', which was the stage at which Lenin wanted to call a halt in 1918. The economy could then comprise a public sector, a mixed sector and a co-operative sector, while the private sector would include at least anything to do with family firms, including a few salaried personnel (farming, craft industries, services, small workshops etc.). By 'relying on their own resources' the authorities would decide to put an end to imports of luxury goods and to slap a very heavy tax on semi-luxury goods. This would enable them to earmark all the money earned by exports (or even funds received in the form of aid, though their policy of neutrality would probably cut down any such aid) for buying any foodstuffs that could not be produced at home, plus raw materials and any pieces of equipment given priority rating by their Plan.

Many of the luxury foods that are now being imported would no longer be bought outside the country, which would open up a wider market for local farmers. The farmers would be given firm protection by the State in the form of credits and expert advice, which would enable them to take advantage of these new markets. A study would be made to determine which types of industry would be necessary to take care of the country's essential needs, equipment would be bought in the light of the results of this study. Purchases of equipment from abroad would be kept to a minimum, which would involve less wastage of mineral resources; and the maximum number of jobs would be open to young people so as to reduce unemployment, which would be the prime target.

There is a danger that intermediate technologies, which require a greater import of manpower than capital and are therefore an important aspect of any economic transformation that is capable of 'standing on its own two feet' would not be competitive internationally. They would therefore be given protection against international competition, at least in the early stages, though this protection must not be abused. They would be expected to give priority to providing equipment for agricultural production and to ordinary consumer products, to the exclusion of luxury goods.

Absolute priority would therefore be given to intensifying agriculture, since it is still the basis of the economy in countries that are not yet fully industrialized; an example here is China, though this fact wasn't recognized there until about 1960. As I have tried to show over and over again, particularly since 1961, this step is absolutely essential if there is to be a cut in food imports, if nutrition is to be improved and the danger of famine removed, if local factories are to get the supplies they need, and the need for foreign currency and thus dependence on others is to be reduced. This type of modernization, which would be to a certain extent modelled on the Chinese example, would start with a new attempt to bring literacy to the great mass of the peasant class on a renewed functional basis, and would continue with the creation of a cadre of technologists, which would also speed up progress. It is not enough simply to learn to read and write and learn a trade. The peasants would have to be made aware of the political conditions of their being made truly free. They could then, by forming themselves into organizations that would be genuinely representative, play an effective part in drawing up plans for production and regional development and in creating co-operative bodies to provide the necessary services. These co-operative bodies would provide credit and the recipients of such credit would be supervised to make sure that they made the best possible use of the money in making improvements to their plant, by using all the country's 'hidden productive resources'. Methods of tilling the soil would be improved and a rational agricultural timetable for crop-growing would be introduced. There would be widespread but judicious use of organic manure, followed by fertilizers and pesticides, many of which (e.g. pyrethrum, rotenone, nicotine) can be produced on the spot and are not harmful; even if they are expensive to produce, they would, which is more important, create new jobs.

The next step – this model is intended first and foremost for tropical Africa – would be to organize the use of draught animals, to integrate agriculture and stock-breeding, which would involve building up stocks of fodder and using manure, ploughs and animal-drawn carts. This could pave the way for the use of chemical fertilizers, on a moderate scale, for improved seeds, for the type of farming appropriate to a country involved in the Green Revolution. Quick-growing trees

85

planted near each village would provide firewood, so that dung (and faeces) could be used as manure.

In most countries intensification along these lines could produce a virtually unlimited supply of manual work. This would be available particularly to young people, whose education, as we shall see later, will be completely rethought. In that case it would be a good idea if members of the peasantry, male and female, were to agree at the same time to give 50 days or so per annum of virtually unpaid labour, as in China. This would involve improvements to the land (water control, measures to combat erosion, reafforestation, planting fruit-trees etc.) and would be seen as a contribution to making the country economically independent, thus creating an uplifting feeling of sacrifice to a higher cause. Better still, they would receive a small fee based on the value of food, which would be in more plentiful supply thanks to the worldwide 'food for peace' programme based on an expected increase in resources. (Solis points out that I am asking the poorest sector of society to do more work.)

At this point the irrigation equipment that turned out, according to the analysis made by the young engineer in the *Génie Rural,* to be ruinously expensive in Niger, would become economically viable. The collectives formed by the peasantry most closely concerned would be completely responsible for the upkeep of such equipment. I can't give any details about how quickly and how intensively agriculture can be put on a 'co-operative' basis within the framework of a system of collective management, since they will depend on a widely varying set of conditions. But most of all they will depend on the degree of collective consciousness arrived at by those doing the work, if – and this is the scheme I opt for – the majority won't be put under any form of constraint.

We have seen the extent of the failures, or at any rate the difficulties created for agriculture in the Soviet Union, Cuba and Eastern Europe by unnecessary constraints. So the first step would be to set up co-operatives to deal with financing, trade and supplies, and services. The process of collectivization would be taken a stage further only if the peasants wanted this, if the appropriate stage of development had been reached, and if it would represent a genuine step forward. The potential of the peasant class, a structure that offers a considerable source of inventiveness, has not yet been exhausted. At this point all the tropical forests, many of which have had their most precious resources 'creamed off', would be gradually replanted artificially. This would ensure that their soil and climate were properly protected. If the wood thus produced is liberally impregnated to stop it rotting, the build-up of carbon means that there will be less carbon dioxide in the atmosphere. At the same time the wood will replace the dwindling supply of metal and the use of plastics, which is far from desirable. Motors that run on producer gas could just as easily run on wood. And, bureaucrats please note, there would be a campaign to prevent wastage of paper!

In the field of pollution the Chinese example could once again be followed in many instances. Some aspects of the Chinese way of coping with the problem can easily be recognized in the list of ideas given in the last paragraph. But I should point out that this doesn't mean that the Chinese political model is the only one that can be followed. (Before thinking that we should have to know more about how exactly it functions at the top, and about the struggle for power that is taking or has taken place in China.)

In the August 1972 issue of the official journal *La Chine en Construction* we are shown how the town of Kirin in Manchuria in north-eastern China produces 70,000 metric tons of cement per annum from the waste matter resulting from the manufacture of calcium carbide; how coal-dust is collected and used for manufacturing bricks (housewives in northern France used to collect it and use it for heating down to 1914 and later); how waste-water which is rich in ammonia is used to fertilize 2,700 hectares of land belonging to the local people's communes, and so on. The point is that the Chinese are industrializing their rural districts without urbanizing them, which means that they can avoid a good many of the difficulties our societies are encountering, and yet still economize on their use of resources.

8    *The second revolt: the setting-up of international boards to handle raw materials*

Whereas the first set of changes of this type can be made on the national level, the battle against increasingly unfair terms of exchange could be waged much more effectively on the basis of international agreement. If the poor nations were united in a common front against the rich nations their negotiating power would be increased. After the failure of Mossadeq's battle in Iran against the oil trusts, which he started fighting in 1951, the trusts were forced to step aside 20 years later, at Teheran and Tripoli in 1971. The first battle is never wasted, even if the outcome is failure, as in the case of the Paris Commune, provided that the lessons of all failures (like those in Mali, Ghana and Guinea) are properly learnt. Even if Iran and Saudi Arabia did later let the group of oil-producing companies off the hook they all got a lot more out of them than they would have if OPEC (the Organization of Petroleum-Exporting Countries) hadn't stepped in. And Algeria could shake off French protection more advantageously.

Over the last few years every copper-producing country has been planning to implement without delay a programme to step up production very considerably. As a result the price of copper has dropped. If Chile, Peru, Zambia and Zaire had got together to draw up an agreement as firm as that of OPEC in 1971–3, and were not now so impatient to rake in large amounts of foreign currency, they would spend time setting up a single marketing organization with a production quota for each country fixed by mutual agreement.

They could settle for a target price of £1000 per metric ton of copper; a price of close on £500 was being quoted in February 1973. A policy of substitution would then be practised more widely, which would mean that more copper would be available for a longer period on the world level. On the other hand, the producing countries that decide to slow down their sales somewhat will have to extend their present period of semi-austerity. But they are virtually certain of being able to get increasingly high prices in the future, since by then the scarcity of copper will be a recognized fact throughout the world; and it will become increasingly scarce.

In my last book[9] I recommended that each of the main tea-exporting countries* should first set up a national tea board with an export monopoly, rather on the model of the British marketing boards. Then comes the second stage, which is the only one that is liable to be effective for products where the supply is far outstripped by demand from people who are in a position to pay for them. The second stage involves setting

* Ceylon, India, China, East Africa, Mauritius, Indonesia and Argentina.

up an international marketing board to be in sole charge of world sales of the product in question, following the sales quotas for each country fixed by general agreement. This would be the best way of allowing the producing countries to keep their end up in the face of the 'oligopolises', the international trusts distributing tea – provided they agreed to a cutback in output, since this is the only sure way of pushing up prices. The poor nations in the Middle East could be given special prices. It's only fair that the rich nations should pay more for the same quality.

A similar scheme could be adopted for the main agricultural and mineral products of the Third World countries, including oil (though there will also have to be a cut in oil consumption). The producing countries would organize themselves into a group before entering into talks with the consuming countries. If they didn't, at any meeting where the two sides got together the consuming countries would take advantage of their technological superiority and of the lack of unity and differing interests of the dominated countries, which would still be too bound up with producing the raw materials.

This scheme doesn't claim to solve all the difficulties. It isn't a universal panacea. And a monopoly of sales doesn't necessarily mean excessively high prices. Whenever the rich nations can produce enough or almost enough for their own needs (as in the case of oil-seeds) or can compete with synthetic products (textiles, rubber etc.), as they did in the nineteenth century in the case of synthetic dyes, the claims of the poor nations will inevitably have to be lower. Yet the negotiating strength of the poor countries would still be vastly improved. Particularly if they cut back intelligently on the amount of crops grown for export, thus both improving their takings (King's Law) and increasing the amount of food available at home.

9 *The third revolt: repudiating excessive debts and nationalizing the subsoil*

Once the common front of the poor nations against the rich nations has been consolidated to a large extent, even embracing countries with different ideologies, a new move can be made. They can refuse to recognize unfair debts they have contracted, which would include the great majority of the dominated countries' obligations, if we agree to take into account factors such as the worsening of terms of trade, the fact that payments for raw materials (the scarcity of which is generally underestimated) have been far too low, the unfair profits that have accrued from commercial transactions, from sales of equipment, technology and diplomas, and from services such as insurance, freight costs, brokerage by the banks etc. When the late President Pompidou announced at Ouagadougou in the Upper Volta that France would waive the thousand million francs due for FIDES (1948–60) there was amazement all round.* No one realized that all that was still outstanding.

If debts of this kind were repudiated on a fairly wide scale the rich countries would have to accept the situation, like it or not. Retaliatory measures should of course be expected, but their extent will depend very largely on the solidarity or otherwise of the exploited nations, much as it does in trade-union conflicts. The countries affected will have to be prepared for a temporary drop in their imports, and will have to accept – as China has since 1949 – a degree of austerity. But without this they would never escape from the system, or from the widespread poverty among working people that it entails.

But the bickerings and rivalries between the super-powers, the role of Europe, which could be less dependent on the United States, and even more the role of China, which has completely shaken off Soviet influence, will allow them to obtain less draconian conditions than those obtaining today. At any rate they surely wouldn't have much to lose. Their lack of foreign currency will force them to make better use of all their hidden productive resources and to find work for all their young people. Imperialist pressures will represent a 'challenge' for the younger generation to take up as they roll up their sleeves and spit on their hands before grabbing their spades, pickaxes and wheelbarrows . . . .

Roughly the same time as the poor countries repudiate their debts will be the logical moment, assuming it seems feasible at the time, to nationalize the major part of the wealth hidden

* FIDES (Fonds d'Investissements pour le développement économique et social) is a fund set up to supply equipment for the overseas territories of the Union Française (*translator's note*).

in the subsoil and the equipment needed to extract it. This will involve copper, tin, zinc and lead mines; deposits of oil, gas, coal and uranium; iron ores, bauxite, phosphates, potassium etc. The idea would be to recover what in all fairness belongs to the nation as a whole, whatever the County Court of Paris has to say. This 'court of first instance', which has never moved on from the stage of the Napoleonic Code, has authorized the attachment of copper in Chile on behalf of American speculators – a verdict that is nothing more nor less than an affront to the dignity of a country that is merely trying to recover its own wealth.

As for the mining and other equipment, Peru and Chile have shown the other countries how to make allowances for the profit margin – which is generally excessively high – enjoyed by all foreign speculators, such as Miferma in Mauritania, Esso-Standard or Anaconda. It seems that Enrico Mattei* really did, as the film made about the affair shows, pay with his life for his impudence in attacking the stranglehold of the oil trusts, which had never before been questioned. Mossadeq† had lost his authority and his freedom over this question. But martyrs and precursors such as these have paved the way for all those who want to shake off the yoke of dependence, and incidentally the fact that it's been weighing them down for so long in no way justifies its existence.

10  Stage 4: *the gradual formation of an overall economic system for the whole planet; accelerated growth in the dominated countries*

Needless to say things won't work out if the model chosen for the transition to various forms of socialism is selected at

* Enrico Mattei, a dynamic and controversial Italian politician, became Extraordinary Commissioner of the Azienda Italiana Petroli (AGIP) in 1945 and virtually founded the Italian petroleum industry, setting up the Ente Nazionale Idrocarburi (ENI) in 1953, of which he was president (*translator's note*).
† Mohammed Mossadeq (1880–1967), prime minister of Iran from 1951 to 1953, prosecuted the oil dispute with the Anglo-Iranian Oil Co., which interrupted production at Abadan for several years and led to a consortium, including BP, taking over production (*translator's note*).

random. We haven't got a proper sense of history and it's only too easy, alas, to predict the imminent collapse of the fascist or semi-fascist solutions (using 'fascist' in the widest sense of the term) that are under way at this very moment in Latin America or Pakistan, India, Burma, Thailand, Indonesia, the Philippines etc. This means that it's quite impossible to state when, or even if, solutions resembling the model outlined above will be put into practice. After all a large number of different models could be roughed out. But we now realize that quite a lot of these would lead to inevitable catastrophe.

If we continue with our theoretical models we must emphasize once again the many reservations that will have to be made concerning their 'feasibility' (to use a term that is treated as a sacred cow at the United Nations), which will depend on the phases that have already been implemented. At this stage of our argument we should in theory have managed to reduce drastically the incidence of political domination, or even to wipe it out altogether, assuming that we had staged the 'three revolts' outlined above. The sequel would therefore depend, if we take our hypothesis a stage further, on the will-power of the states that have achieved genuine independence. (I shall assume – since the two factors are linked – that they have also managed to muzzle their privileged minorities, though this is easier said than done.) This situation would therefore justify the term 'stage'; a group of states that would never again be under foreign domination would aim to reach this stage – though the fact of being their own masters wouldn't automatically turn them into angels overnight!

The great majority of the exportable oil supplies – and oil is a prime source of energy as things stand at the moment – belongs to countries that are very underpopulated, ranging from Venezuela to Iran, via Libya, Algeria and most of all the Middle East. All these countries taken together have only 100 million inhabitants. A power tax would have a particularly serious effect on oil products, which are liable to be in short supply. In the terms of our model it would be a lot higher than the taxes in force today. And part of the proceeds of the supplementary tax could be refunded to the oil-producing nations, while the rest went to a new fund set up to promote international development.

A similar tax could be levied on metals, with a higher rate for the ones that are likely to become scarce in the near future. This would discourage people from wasting the Earth's scarce resources on such a scale and would also enable the developing countries to get hold of more resources. They could get enough to enable them, particularly once they've cancelled out their debts, to have so much equipment that they would at last be in a position to grow faster than the developed countries, for whom I should incidentally recommend zero growth of global consumption in the near future. But who will collect and distribute these taxes? This will no doubt have to be worked out in a series of different phases.

11 *Centralized allocation of scarce resources; a world economic system rather than world government*

Taking this series of proposals as our starting-point, with on the one hand international marketing boards and on the other a range of *international* taxes on the same raw materials and scarce resources, we would reach the point of working out a system for setting up by gradual stages an economic system on a worldwide scale. This would be easier to put into practice than, and ultimately preferable to, a genuine world government. If the necessary protection is to be afforded to climates (which can be tampered with in the future, bringing an increased threat of dangerous atmospheric disturbance), and to lakes and rivers bordering on the various countries running through them, and particularly to the seas and the atmosphere, a worldwide organization endowed with concrete powers, in other words a supranational authority, will have to be set up. General de Gaulle remained attached to the nineteenth century, the age of nationalities. The time has come to shake off this idea.

The economic aspect of our model could have a similar function to that of the Ministry of Supply in wartime. Our planet is being subjected by the rest of the universe to a *de facto* blockade. Though we are only just beginning to grasp the situation, this will force us one day to set up a centralized system for allocating scarce resources. This would take the justified needs of each national group into account, on a pro rata basis according to their present population figures (with

93

no extra allowance for any population increase) rather than, as now, on the basis of how much they can afford. Under this system the United States would be given, say, 6 per cent of the available supplies of the most important raw materials, or maybe less if the fact that their equipment is already further advanced than in other countries were taken into account, plus their own abundant resources.

One major difficulty in planning on the global scale begins to emerge if we study the way today's 'socialist' economic systems function, or the recent Jackson Report on the UN. The problem is bureaucracy, that scourge of the modern era, which is liable to increase in parallel with the scale of the action taken along these lines. We should therefore aim not to control the world's economic system but to regulate the supply of resources – which won't be so easy. A mushroom growth of international bodies is essential if the necessary emphasis is to be put on decentralization and on evolving self-government. There will inevitably be a number of contra-dictions between these two imperatives, each of which is indispensable, since one calls for a series of global decisions while the other requires that the majority of decisions should be decentralized. 'Highly centralized planning and widely decentralized production' is how Sicco Mansholt puts it.

At every turn local, national and global interests will diverge – hence the need for arbitration. Let's leave the worry as to how to resolve these inevitable contradictions to our grand-children, who will have to bear the full brunt of such prob-lems. We've got quite enough problems of our own to be going on with. But we mustn't make it impossible for these grandchildren to survive, or even more difficult. But don't let's go on painting a hopeful picture of some perfect form of communism with no more contradictions or conflict, a sort of golden age, an earthly paradise – ultimately more Christian than Marxist in inspiration – in which each of us would be able to gratify his desires, which he would call his needs.

Yet the major difficulties will result from the whole series of moves that will have to be made to smooth the transition to whatever form of socialism has been chosen by each country. It is relatively easy to imagine ways of changing the team in power, of taking power away from the privileged minorities, by exploiting the contradictions in the present system and not shrinking from certain types of violence. The Club of Rome's 'revelations' will enable us to isolate the privileged few under the present system even further, by shouting from the rooftops that they are leading *all of us* to catastrophe. But it wouldn't do if their successors snatched power only to abuse it in their turn, which is what happens all the time.

We shall also have to change people, the first to suffer being the mass of us semi-privileged beings – and that includes many ordinary working people in the rich countries. How can we make them accept the disciplines that will very soon become essential if we are to achieve, as we must, zero growth in world consumption? How do we make this zero growth seem more acceptable, and even ultimately pleasanter, than the idea of alienating all those who always want more and yet more and are busy killing themselves at the wheels of their cars?

There you have the crux of the debate about the socialism of tomorrow, about the various different faces it can take on, and ultimately about the future of our 'little planet'. Before tackling these very difficult problems we must look into ways of guarding against the main consequences of the threats that we can now glimpse much more clearly. These consequences will take shape in the near future and the threats that will give rise to them hang heavily over our future – by which I mean the future of the so-called developed countries, which could more truthfully be called the 'selfish and unfair nations'.

I shall therefore try in Part IV, more and more haltingly – but there's no getting out of it now – to rough out a series of measures that appear to be essential in the rich countries, before tackling in Part V (but not solving) some of the political aspects of the problem. I shall ask, for instance, what methods we should use to make the majority of 'have-nots' accept solutions that are often more revolutionary than those put forward by our so-called 'revolutionary parties'. Equally, how can we impose these solutions on the privileged minority of 'haves'?

It's not very likely that we shall succeed. But I still think that since we are rushing head first at a brick wall we'd do better to slow down a bit too soon than much too late. The monetary troubles we're experiencing represent the amber light – which will soon be turning red!

95

Part IV

# GENERAL MOBILIZATION FOR OPERATION SURVIVAL IN THE SELFISH RICH COUNTRIES

1 *A series of non-communist Utopias; we must adopt a different attitude towards the dominated countries*

Up to now I've always avoided speaking in terms of the distant future, since I felt that our ideas about such a future could only get vaguer. I still think that. We really can't see properly what's going to happen when the next 15 years are up, yet here we are rushing headlong into a blanket of fog. We must therefore both cut down our speed (growth) and try to find some stronger headlights (a first step towards working out a global economic system). These interconnected threats have become so serious that we must look for ways of reducing them, if not averting them altogether. Even if, given the present state of public opinion, measures of this kind *still* seem unacceptable to the majority of our fellow-citizens, we must prepare them – after all, they soon won't have any choice but to accept.

For I am now going to study some of the ways in which we can build what Tibor Mende has called 'A Possible World', though this is an increasingly difficult problem. We must also remember that it isn't necessarily the most logical structures that will be adopted. This new world is not and will never be a rational structure. Rather it will be an arena of confrontation and struggle, constantly devising compromises. If there's one thing that's certain it's that no one can predict what the future holds: 'Communism is not what such-and-such a member of the proletariat wants or believes . . . but what he will be historically compelled to do, in accordance with his own being.'[1] This phrase coined by Marx and Engels seems to me thoroughly out of date, particularly in view of the fact that

97

a profusion of supplies, which is an essential pre-condition of that type of communism, is no longer desirable. This in no way absolves us from being concerned about the future, from studying what it may be able to offer. The second thing we can be certain of is that as the future is not subject to pre-determination and obeys no known law it has no fixed meaning. This means that we can exercise a very considerable influence over it, particularly if we form ourselves into groups. If I didn't believe this I should have laid down my pen long ago.

The situation I have outlined in the preceding paragraph involves first of all a complete change of attitude on the part of the selfish rich countries towards the countries that are at present dominated. Rather than giving them advice that is only too often inappropriate – which is no doubt what I've just been doing – it would be better, as Don Helder Camara suggests, to set them an example by reconstructing our own economic system in such a way that we could help them to develop.

Various ideas have been put forward: that their debts should be cancelled; that equipment and social amenities to a value of 5 per cent of our GNPs should be handed over free; that the raw materials market should be organized on a worldwide basis; that food imports in the dominated countries should be cut, and malnutrition reduced; that we should create better openings on our markets for their agricultural produce (oil-seeds, fruit juices, preserved foods, sugar, meat), which should if possible be transformed, and should pay a higher rate for it; and that this should apply even more to their industrial products (textiles, leather, furniture, electronic equipment, toys), and so on. All these ideas, which were put forward long ago but have rarely been implemented, would represent the first stage of a complete change of direction, which would be preceded by a fuller awareness of the situation. The likelihood of a whole series of measures such as these being able to close the gap between us and the dominated countries would be strengthened by the fact that I am going to recommend that consumption of the industrial goods produced by the rich countries should be halted throughout the world.

The report drawn up by the FAO for its regional European conference in Munich in September 1972 reveals that the less developed countries' share of the world export figures for agricultural produce fell from 46 per cent in 1955 to 34 per cent in 1970. The organization's director-general, A. Boerma, criticizes 'the expensive policies designed to hold prices that have been put into effect by the developed countries . . . which have improved the economic situation of the chief exploiting nations', whereas 'the incomes of small-scale farmers remain unacceptably low'. If they increased their agricultural imports from the poor countries by 4 thousand million dollars between now and 1980 this would make a difference of less than 1 per cent to their imports, which are expected to be of the order of 500 thousand million dollars by 1980.

At the same time we should still have to give all these poor countries the means to step up their agricultural output to such an extent that the increased volume of exports won't rob them of their own daily bread and rice, which is what would happen if it continued to be achieved at the expense of food-crops. It seems to me more urgent that they should eat better and be able to supply raw materials to their factories; to cut down their imports and develop their own home market. If the first priority is given to exports, which is the view currently taken by the United Nations, this encourages them to integrate more and more with the world market – which promptly exploits them. This soon gives rise to surpluses, which ruin the poor countries while working to the advantage of the rich consumer nations.

A second stage would lead us to accept a system whereby the allocation of scarce resources was gradually centralized and organized on a world basis. This would involve rationing the main raw materials. The most difficult bit will be finding a way of putting such a wide range of measures into practice, including a radical change of direction in our economic system, in our industrial and agricultural output and in world trade, without bringing about a world economic crisis of the first magnitude and an appalling level of unemployment. We shall probably have to decentralize economic planning for each nation step by step, though the exact course that this process will take has yet to be worked out. It would at any rate be controlled by the various world bodies that I have already referred to. We shall have to work out a clear-cut political line for these various institutions, which will have to be specified when the time comes. I shall merely put forward a few rough outlines, since it is not up to me to decide, and anyway the time is not yet ripe.

2   *Zero population growth in the rich countries and in world consumption of their industrial products*

The need to halt population growth, which will soon become necessary throughout the world, is thus, as I have shown, a matter of much greater urgency in the rich countries, which have a much higher level of wastage and pollution than the other countries. If we could reduce inequality we could put a stop to maternity allowances and could follow up with taxes designed to slow down the birth-rate, leading eventually to authoritarian restrictions and a fixed quota of births for each of the rich countries. If we added to this the stage-by-stage population shifts that are dictated by both history and geography, so that, for instance, people moved from northern China and Japan to Siberia, or from southern China, India, Bengal and Pakistan to Australasia, Sumatra, North and South America and tropical Africa, there would be no under-populated countries left anywhere in the world.

The developed countries could then initiate a series of measures, which would be put into effect on a step-by-step basis to avoid widespread unemployment, to reorganize their economies so as to achieve zero growth in world consumption of industrial products. This does not in any way imply that production should be brought to a halt. Firstly, we shall have to manufacture an increasing amount of industrial equipment and provide increasing quantities of fertilizers etc. for the poor countries (until such time as they are able to manufacture their own, in the factories we give them). The poor countries would thus no longer be dominated, in that we would *give* them whatever they need most.

Halting our global industrial consumption would not perpetuate the poverty at present experienced by the elderly, by immigrant workers and by young people unable to find work. I am strongly in favour of population shifts on a still wider scale, provided that the new immigrant labour is given proper training in the host countries. Assuming that the level of global industrial output will remain the same as far as internal consumption goes, a greater concern for social justice should ensure that the goods are much more evenly distributed, both at home and abroad. Housing and food supplies could be less dependent on industry. Since the level of industrial output would be fixed, it could and must be distributed much more fairly, though the new restrictions resulting from the centralized allocation and rationing of scarce resources that will soon be put into effect will have to be taken into account.

The first step would be to tax luxury goods (e.g. large cars) increasingly heavily; at a later stage those that do the most damage or waste the most money would be banned altogether. Some articles in this group are also extremely non-functional and the process of manufacturing them creates an even higher level of pollution. Lastly, and here we come to the most frightening problem of all, some of them represent the greatest possible threat to our survival. Thus if we are to survive we must use every means at our disposal to put an end to them in the shortest possible time. I'm sure you'll have guessed that I'm talking about arms, nuclear arms and even conventional weapons.

3   *There must be a cutback in arms production, followed by a total ban; this will devalue the individual nation to a certain extent*

Arms, particularly nuclear arms, are the most serious threat of all, by the very fact of their existence. They waste labour, space, energy and scarce minerals; they create a dangerous level of air and water pollution; they cause leukaemia and may cause other forms of genetic disturbance that are not as yet fully recognized. We are quite clearly struggling more and more in the dark, against a danger that may well jeopardize our future. Industrial waste that is still radioactive is going to pose an increasingly difficult problem, and an increasingly dangerous one.

The 12 October, 1972 issue of *Politique-Hebdo* printed an impressive photograph of some of the 18,000 blocks of concrete in which the radioactive waste from the nuclear powerhouse at Saclay is locked up: 500 of them have already been cracked or otherwise damaged by frost. The waste is going to be taken by road to The Hague, which will take 5 years according to the plans for road-transport that have been drawn up! If it went by train it would cost less and would take only 3 years. The journal *Survivre et Vivre*\* has stressed the danger this represents.

Peaceful coexistence between all nations, whether or not they possess arms, has become absolutely essential for survival. But it must go hand in hand with respect for the weakest. I was asked to take part in a conference organized in May 1970 by the Quaker group at the United Nations, which was to be attended by 16 'wise men' from all over the world. The subject was the one that concerns us here: 'On Human Survival'. The subcommission detailed to deal with the question of 'war and peace' discussed arms restrictions, particularly among the Americans and the Soviets (I was going to say among gentlemen), and they tackled this question with great seriousness, treating it as purely theoretical, as if it were timeless. I threatened to leave the conference and slam the door behind me if they went on refusing to discuss Vietnam and the Middle East. 'But we'll never accept your views on Vietnam!' 'That's no excuse for the way you're apparently ignoring it, as though it were some shameful disease' – and anyway it *was* a shameful disease!

Ordinary working people are not sufficiently concerned about disarmament. A statement that 'progressive and simultaneous research' is being carried out into the whole question of disarmament is enough to wipe out any possibility of ever achieving it. To destroy all nuclear weapons would be a first and positive step, and indeed the only way of preventing them from proliferating to a dangerous extent. Unilateral disarmament of the kind recommended to the French people by Louis Lecoin would undeniably give the first country who dared to take such a step great international prestige, yet France is continuing her nuclear tests.

Each nation is planning to survive, at least in its present form, and claims to be justified in so doing. Some nations, Israel for instance, are trying to widen their boundaries, and indeed many boundaries are completely irrational, or at any rate this goes for those that are a legacy of imperialism. Yet if their validity were questioned this would give rise to endless conflicts. What we could do, however, is to make an attempt to devalue these boundaries little by little, since they are so artificial and their origins are so questionable, by gradually lessening the most dangerous forms of national sovereignty.

\* 5 rue Thorel, Paris 2e.

A nation is made up of a series of provinces, many of which were attached to the others by means of bloodshed.

In France P. Carrer reminded us recently of:

> The Crusade against the Catharians, which reached its height when the castle of Montsegur was burned down, and which saw the lands that spoke the *langue d'Oc*, which had a more advanced civilization than that of their northern conquerors, being terrorized into submission. The wild scenes of the conquest of the Duchy of Burgundy, whose passionately anti-French inhabitants fought desperately against Louis XI's troops in 1479, after the death of Charles the Rash . . . . We should also mention the six thousand Bretons who died at Saint-Aubin-de-Cormier in 1488 for their country's independence, which was shortly to end after surviving for eight hundred years.[2]

We really must pull these chauvinistic myths to pieces!

World unity could not be achieved at the cost of armed clashes on this scale throughout the planet without leading to mass suicide. So while a ban on arms does not mean that individual nations must disintegrate – that's not the way they'll end – they will have to watch their authority as aggressors dwindling. This would lead to the setting up of a supranational authority, which would have to be invested with enough powers to be able to *impose* arbitration and to end conflicts. Although the United Nations was set up to do just this it does not have any real authority, and has therefore so far proved to be more or less incapable of doing so.

4 *A redistribution of wealth; international taxation; and an end to the horrors of the assembly line*

If this devaluation and cutback of the authority of individual nations were achieved in relation to other nations it would be easier to reduce their powers of coercion at home as well. This could be achieved if society were not so hierarchical, since one of the basic functions of the constraints in force today is to perpetuate unwarrantable inequalities. A widespread acceptance of the semi-austerities that I shall be examining would scarcely be compatible with a continuance of the blatant injustices in the rich countries today, with their wide range of incomes, which allows the better-off to squander money and resources to the point of sheer folly – or even ridicule, though this doesn't in any way lessen their insolence or the harm they cause.

We shall have to cut down all this waste and then stop it altogether, starting with a campaign of reform which could be the prelude to a revolutionary transformation of society, or at any rate could dig deeper without causing any serious violence. Our aim would be to avoid mass unemployment during the period of transition to a survival economy. This would necessitate an increasing level of taxation, which would become progressively prohibitive, on all the most wasteful and ostentatious forms of luxury, and on all those that create a high level of pollution. Examples are private yachts and planes used purely for pleasure; stately homes and luxury second homes; flashy cars; private game reserves etc. And we should have to bring in very heavy income tax for the wealthiest among us, at the same time exposing the widespread tax-evasion in France that the British and Americans find so amazing.

A wealth tax would also have to be brought in, particularly on excess capital, and estate duty would have to be increased. A fixed proportion of the sums raised by these taxes would go into various funds for international development. This basic idea of an international levy is beginning to gain ground in United Nations circles. It could turn out to be the first step towards setting up a world economic system, with the help of the emotional response to the environment question.

The effect of putting an end to these non-essential activities, including arms production, would be to free huge quantities of scarce metals and qualified labour. This would make it possible to cut down the amount of labour needed very considerably, particularly with the anticipated rises in production, and would at the same time allow the sectors of society that are currently underprivileged to enjoy greater resources, both at home and abroad. With a fairer distribution of incomes and an across-the-board rise for the lowest-paid workers the poorest sectors could eat and dress better and educate their children better, while at the same time new possibilities would be opened up for agriculture at home and abroad and for all trades. Don't tell me it can't be done – in Iceland a waitress in a café earns the equivalent of £150 per month, a minister earns £200 and a trawler captain £250. This means that the range of salaries is even narrower than in China! The Grenelle agreement of May 1968 could have made a start towards making salary structures less 'hierarchical'.*

If all building land were handed over to the municipal authorities this would stop the speculators in their tracks. If all funds available were allocated to low-cost housing this would halt the creeping canker of luxury villas – the reverse side of that particular coin is the shanty-town. There seems no reason why each family should have its own set of electric appliances.

In Ottawa, which is a richer town than any in France, large blocks of flats have communal washing machines, which each family can use as often as they want merely by putting 25 cents in the slot and then loading the machine with their own washing and detergent. Yet a more radical transformation of our present way of life would require all of us to become aware of the situation in the very near future and to accept fully, before it's too late, the unarguable fact that most of our resources are going to be in short supply from now on – which would force us to draw our own conclusions about what must be done.

As we shall see, this semi-austerity wouldn't be purely a matter of constraints and restrictions. In fact I'm probably wrong to use the word 'austerity' at all. We certainly shouldn't allow the sort of waste that increases the poverty of the poor countries. But on the other hand we should expect people to work much less hard. There would no longer be any justification for the hellish rhythms of assembly-line production, where you have to work faster and faster all the time, or for the soul-destroying work of 'specialist workers', who are responsible for just one tiny bit of the production process, or of immigrant labour. A drop in output and increased automation would not put more people out of work but would instead give greater leisure all round, once society decides to give the first priority to distributing all the work that still needs to be done on a fair and rational basis. This would

* On 26 May, 1968 representatives of the employers and trade union federations accepted Pompidou's offer of talks with the government on wage structures and other problems hotly debated during the disturbances; the talks were held at the Hôtel du Châtelet in the rue de Grenelle, in the ministerial quarter, and after nearly 30 hours' acrimonious discussions lasting into 27 May a tentative agreement was drawn up (*translator's note*).

necessitate creating new types of economic decision-making authority and freeing the economy from the profit motive....
I realize that this is easier said than done, but I must still start by saying it, pointing out that work can become a real pleasure if there is less of it, if it has been organized differently, so that it is more varied and is distributed by each individual team of workers.

### 5 A Blockade Ministry; a power tax and a raw materials tax, with recycling of resources

A 'Blockade Ministry' similar to the one entrusted to Georges Monnet by the French President of the Council of Ministers, Édouard Daladier, in September 1939, might speed up the public awareness of the gravity of the situation that is so urgently needed. An institution of this kind, which suggests a state of war, would by its very name be liable to stir the imagination of the general public. If each nation – the rich ones first – were to set up a Blockade Ministry, which would be a logical corollary to the Department of the Environment, it would encourage the general public to grasp more quickly – and speed is of the essence – the need to set up the world body to allocate scarce resources on the centralized basis that I outlined above.

For the intermediary stage, which could be put into effect immediately, as a means of making the transition to a socialist society geared to survival, I should like to refer to the *Ecologist* group in Britain, who recommend that taxes should be levied to encourage people to save scarce resources, as I have already indicated (see Part III, section 10): 'A raw materials tax . . . designed to enable our reserves to last over an arbitrary period of time, the longer the better . . . . This tax would penalize resource-intensive industries and favour employment-intensive ones . . . . [It] would obviously encourage recycling . . . .'[3]

The metal from American planes shot down over Vietnam was immediately salvaged, whereas our 'car cemeteries' are nothing but useless and sordid heaps of refuse. The rate of taxation could soon be fixed at a level at which it would become financially worth while to salvage the metal from abandoned cars, and to recycle all our so-called 'rubbish'.

Bertrand de Jouvenel sensibly reminded me that we've never struck gold in our dustbins. If measures of this kind were put into effect the day would soon come when we wouldn't even find any tin in them – in the early days of the century we in France used to collect bits of tin from the fields to make knives and forks, and make a collection during the catechism to 'ransom' little Chinese girls who were left to die – or zinc, or lead or copper. Second-hand dealers, scrap-merchants and rag-and-bone men dealing in metal would be given a new lease of life (the latter used to collect rabbit-skins in the days when rabbit-hutches flourished in every back yard). In the Hitler period the Germans used to put their rubbish in separate containers (one for vegetable peelings to be used as pigfeed, one for paper, one for metal and one for everything else).

My British colleagues recommended a power tax, which would encourage people to economize on resources and would be a brake on pollution: 'This would penalize power-intensive processes and hence those causing considerable pollution.'[4] They also recommend an amortization tax,

> ...which would be proportionate to the estimated life of the product, e.g. it would be 100 per cent for products designed to last no more than a year, and would then be progressively reduced to zero per cent for those designed to last 100 + years. Plastics, for example, which are so remarkable for their durability, would be used only in products where this quality is valued, and not for single-trip purposes.[5]

Plastics are beginning to replace metal for a large number of uses where durability is desirable, and this should be en-couraged in all instances where they will not produce harmful results. For instance, they shouldn't be used for blood transfusions, since this has already caused accidents.

The shortage of water and electricity could be lessened by the use of a graduated fee-scale whereby the upper levels of consumption in each household would pay increasingly high rates. This is exactly the opposite of what happens now in France, where the poor are compelled to pay for a minimum consumption, generally 60 cubic metres of water per annum, even if they don't use it. Everyone would be more careful about turning off the light and the air-conditioning equipment every time they went out of a room than the people of Quebec are today. People would often have showers instead of baths and the use of special soaps or detergents should enable waste water to be used for irrigation; this would minimize the conflict between the urban authorities and the rural population for the use of water. 'As far as industry is concerned, the net effect would be to encourage the installation of closed-circuit systems for water . . . .'[6]

If we don't put measures of this kind into operation we shall be forced to build dams and reservoirs all over the place and to drown all our valleys.[7] And in the end we shall still be short of water for our essential needs. The possibility of wrapping icebergs round the poles in insulating plastic and transporting them elsewhere is being examined; the first calculations suggest that the water that could be added to the oceans by this method would work out cheaper than present supplies in California. This might be an attractive solution, though it could be only temporary, since the 'capital' of water accumulated is a non-renewable resource, as is fossil water pumped up from a great depth (e.g. in the Sahara). Once it has been used up we'd have to make do with the 'income' represented by the newly formed ice.

The Blockade Ministry, which would also be responsible for dealing with imports and local production and the use of scarce resources, would publish periodic statements of how things were going on the various 'battle-fronts'. Current French policy seems to be showing very little concern about these threats, which the government refused to believe in. This irresponsible attitude is liable to be judged very severely by their grandchildren.

In view of these various shortages, if it were generally accepted that our objective is genuine social justice throughout the world the whole of our economic policy would have to be revised. It's virtually impossible to deal with all the various aspects of it, since many of them will not appear until certain events, many of which cannot be foreseen, have occurred. But it does look as though we can take certain urgent steps. I feel that these must be taken where the most obvious symbol of our society in its most marked phase of pollution and waste is concerned – I refer of course to the private car. I have already emphasized the harm it does (see Part II, section 3).

Our towns are going to become increasingly impossible to
live in, yet this state of affairs cannot be measured by our
GNP, since this includes on the credit side even the amount of
petrol used up during traffic-jams, whereas this should of
course be entered on the debit side, as should the figures for
the numbers of dead and injured and those who suffer
permanent disablement, plus the cost of repairing cars involved in accidents (which is also seen as swelling the various
GNPs!). A. Sauvy has exposed the exorbitant privileges
bestowed on private cars and road-haulage lorries in France.
In October 1972 we were told that road traffic was for the
first time heavier than goods traffic by rail. And lorries with a
capacity of 38 metric tons are being allowed to damage our
roads. The tremors they set up, which are more like earth-
quakes, are destroying the Colosseum in Rome, Milan
Cathedral and even the Panthéon in Paris. To these 'privileges'
we must add the most important of all: the right to create
clouds of pollution to degrade the atmosphere. We really
must hit back before it's too late.

Our aim should be to penalize the private car in various
ways, the idea being to cut down the increase in the number
of cars and later to cut down the actual number on the roads.
The principal reason for this is that, according to Aurelio
Peccei, one of the top men at Fiat, the private car takes up
'25 times as much urban land per capita as public transport'.[8]
So we shouldn't boast, as Helmut Schmidt did on 22 September 1972, the day when the Brandt cabinet was scuttled,
that whereas in 1969 a manual worker had to put in 1,000
hours of work before he could afford a Volkswagen, in 1972
650 hours' worth would do it! The new aerotrain running
between Paris and Lyon will use up 9 litres of diesel-oil to
transport a passenger 440 kilometres in 2 hours, in complete
safety.

The first step would be to make it very much more expensive to buy a private car, by raising the VAT on it; as a
rough figure we might increase the cost by at least a factor of
3, multiplying by 10 for large cars. The road tax would be
much higher for the first few years in the life of a car, and
would then go down every year, dropping by rapid stages
after 5 years until no tax was payable at all after 10 years. The

idea would be to encourage manufacturers to produce a narrower range of much simpler but very hard-wearing cars, and to give car-maintenance firms an incentive to maintain them better. If this system were put into operation petrol tax would also go up. We know that during this period the cost of extracting oil and the higher dues on it, which will be going up rapidly all the time – there's already a shortage in the United States! – will add to these higher costs.

At the same time a proportion of the taxes levied would be used to subsidize all the various forms of public transport, particularly those that don't cause pollution, such as trolley-buses, trams and electric trains. The cost of running a private car will have to be made so expensive that it would be very much cheaper to travel by train, even for a group of 4 or 5 people. An outing by car must become a real luxury. Bicycles would also be subsidized and there would be no road tax on motorcycles that caused a low level of pollution and presented little danger (i.e. those with a cylinder capacity of under 50 cc and a maximum speed of less than 50 kilometres an hour).

Large numbers of express coaches, which would soon be electric, would serve a wide network of country routes. Once urban traffic congestion had been eased electric trams and trolley-buses would enable everyone to travel quickly all over our towns without using a private car. They would be free, so non-users would pay their share by means of the rates. (Incidentally, in towns such as Paris, where ticket-punchers are stuck underground all day in the Metro, this system would free them from their prison.) Electric cars are already being used in Dijon, and Florence is thinking of putting hire bicycles at the disposal of all residents. Free private parking could and should be banned in the centre of all towns, which in the case of Paris would mean more than half its present surface area. The cost of metred parking would go up by stages until it was pretty well prohibitive, and ultimately it would be banned altogether.

During the second stage private cars would be banned altogether except in cases of justified need and during specific hours (morning deliveries and collecting purchases in the afternoon etc.). The aim would be to restrict the town centre to public transport, lorries, fire-engines, taxis, ambulances etc. The underground network would be extended and improved at the same time, so that it could offer the same sort of comfort as the RER.* With working hours shorter and both working hours and holidays staggered the idiotic traffic congestion that now builds up would be reduced and leisure facilities could be used more extensively. At a later stage the only private vehicles allowed in towns would be electric cars.

On roads outside towns the privileges now enjoyed by road-haulage firms would be stopped, since they give these 'public poisoners' a great advantage over the railways. In the case of France virtually all the fruit and vegetables grown in the main producing areas (i.e. the Rhône Valley, the Garonne and Loire regions, Brittany and Roussillon) could be transported by rail to the new central market of Rungis outside Paris, or to the other large consuming centres. Express trains would jolt the produce a good deal less and would keep it at least as fresh as when it went by road. It would be logical to organize a system whereby lorries worked in conjunction with rail transport, collecting produce from stations and delivering it, with containers making the whole process simpler. They would also be used for connections with local centres, for agricultural transport or for local markets at new stations-cum-markets, which would have become the most important centres for selling, sorting, packing and despatching produce.

For transporting all heavy materials – bricks, tiles, stone, coal, coke, ore – we can make more extensive use of the canals, which we shall have to make deeper, and the railway. The new turbotrain, the high-powered electric train and later the aero-train would speed up transport and, most important of all, would cause less pollution and be much safer than any motorway. At the same time the installation costs would be lower for the same volume of traffic, they would swallow up fewer green spaces, crop-bearing fields and recreation grounds and would thus allow a larger amount of oxygen to be produced. This policy could also justify the existence of secondary railway lines, since it's only because of the exorbitant privileges granted to road transport and private cars that the rail boards have recently been forced into axing them.

A depot from which bikes, electric motorbikes and electric cars could be hired would be set up in each station, so that

* The Réseau Express Régional (RER) is the new rapid line running right across Paris from Saint-Germain-en-Laye in the north-west to Créteil in the south-east, thus extending the Metro network further than ever before (*translator's note*).

people could get home quickly. Bikes, motorbikes and self-drive electric taxis could later be available to the general public in each town. If we want to go in for more and more travelling – in the United States the average member of the public spends over a fifth of his income on travelling – we must, in Peccei's words, 'cut down on other items in the cost of living and in particular introduce draconian birth-control measures'.

In the meantime the number of pedestrian footpaths and cycle tracks, like those in the Netherlands, should be increased without delay. Thus the people who cause no pollution and waste no power, and will therefore be entitled to all the community benefits going, will be able to get about freely, without, as now, constantly running the risk of being killed by hit-and-run drivers, who take unfair advantage of society, pollute needlessly and place little value on the lives of others. In the suburbs of Ottawa I took my life in my hands by going to the supermarket on foot – which my Quebec friends thought a completely ridiculous idea.

7  *A cutback in air travel, which will have to be rationalized*

The fact that more and more members of the rich nations are travelling by air at increasing speeds represents a danger for our climates and reserves of resources that will soon be difficult to accept. Each jet aeroplane leaves trails of vapour behind it, and the build-up of cloud over the Atlantic appears to have increased very considerably since transatlantic flights became so common. The first to go would be flights by military personnel, who are always sending their machines with their unprecedented potential for massacre flying around all over the place, at vast cost to the taxpayer. The fuel that is wasted on such exercises, which quite apart from being completely unprofitable leave a terrible threat hanging over our heads, will no longer be available to our descendants. They'll have good grounds for complaining of our short-sightedness – or rather they'll probably call it our lunacy.

I have already spoken out against the Concorde and the

other supersonic aeroplanes – a bit late in the day, since they didn't enter into my usual field of work – because they use up much more fuel per passenger and therefore cause at least three times as much pollution. Which is quite disproportionate to the short amount of time 'saved'. They will demolish the layer of ozone that protects us at a great height from the deadly ultraviolet rays. No one is precious enough to justify taking this sort of risk, with the possible exception of a messenger bearing news of a threat to peace. In 1971 and 1972 I crossed the Atlantic in a jumbo-jet. Less than a third or even a quarter of the 350 seats were filled, but that didn't mean that the plane burned up less petrol. So it must have used 3 or 4 times as much fuel per passenger as was really necessary.

Competition between the various airlines is clearly a good thing for the passenger, since he gets better service. But from the point of view of the future of mankind we are entitled to think of such a passenger, with his insistence on a fixed timetable and a high level of comfort, as making exorbitant demands. If the various airlines got together to agree on an international system for rationalizing travel on the busiest routes, planes would not have to leave until all their seats were filled, even if this involved delays in some cases.

This would mean making greater use of the charter system, whereby the earlier you decide on your departure date and buy your ticket the less it would cost you. The businessman who decided to travel at the last moment would pay more for this privilege. But there must be a cutback in all types of air travel so as to save on scarce resources and to lessen damage to the atmosphere. Cheap flights can for this reason be seen as highly dangerous. It's true of course that travel broadens the minds of the young, but others are going to go in for exoticism in a big way and exploit the poverty of the local people by buying up their goods cheap and taking advantage of the local girls. And the opportunities for this kind of thing will be restricted to the rich nations, giving them yet another set of privileges.

Private planes would have to be discouraged first of all, at least as firmly as large private cars, since their level of pollution and the effect they have on the climate is liable to become intolerable in the near future, if their numbers continue to increase at the same rate. Congestion over airports is already causing insoluble problems and necessitating long waits (which are unprofitable and dangerous and cause unnecessary pollution) before planes can land, greater risk of collisions and an endless series of landing fields, which are wasting more and more land all the time.

If all the planned schemes for improving the whole communications network of roads, railways, canals, airports, harbours etc., and for building schools, hospitals and so on, and for increasing output, were put end to end, or rather side by side, by the end of next century there would be scarcely any green spaces left at all – as witness California. The time has come to plan further ahead, rather than continuing to waste our resources, *all* of which are finite, without counting the cost. Even clean air, which the classic economics textbooks used to give as an example of a commodity that had no value, because it was thought to be unlimited. In fact its quality is going down as fast as its value is going up . . . .

## 8 *Putting the brakes on unchecked urbanization*

The monster town symbolizes a series of dangers that are highly alarming as far as our future is concerned. If we continue to cause more and more pollution all of us will try to escape one day. The smart suburbs are full of attractive houses surrounded by big gardens, but the people who live in them are having to travel increasingly long distances to get to their place of work, and are thus causing an even higher level of pollution. Satellite towns built further away and on a more rational basis would cut down some of these disadvantages, but we should probably have to go a stage further and discourage all forms of urbanization, as the Chinese do. They are attempting to restrict the urban population to 110 or 120 million and are therefore forcing most of their schoolchildren to join 'people's communes' in the rural districts.

The idea of living close to nature is becoming increasingly popular. Instead of today's long distances (for the rich!) between one's place of work and one's home, an effort could be made to bring the two closer together by creating more and more jobs and setting up more and more plants or businesses in small or medium-sized towns, rural centres and even villages. Tax incentives would help here. This would mean that the holiday homes at present owned by people who live in large towns such as Paris or Marseilles could be raised to the level of first homes. The new country-dwellers would hardly ever go into the nearest town, except for entertainment and for buying certain articles. This would lessen traffic congestion in large built-up areas.

A more intensive programme of cultural activities could be organized in small market towns in country districts, and in smaller towns in the second rank. Teachers, engineering executives, doctors, some retired people and so on would be able to organize and initiate interesting discussions on the major economic, cultural or political questions of the day, such as the best way to help immigrants and under-developed communities to shake off their poverty; or the future of the large town and the effects of giving a new lease of life to the regions; or the idea of discouraging chauvinism and the subsequent effect on the future of nations and on the world, plus the type of worldwide bodies that should be thought up. A growing number of people would be able to appreciate the arts. For instance what is generally known as 'abstract' art is only really a form of decoration and is thus available to everyone. Everyone can decorate his own home with a bit of wood and a few paints, just as everyone can plant his own garden, thus creating a real work of art. He can go in for a Japanese garden or an Italian, French or English one as he fancies, and depending on how much space he has.

Every single square metre of land must be turned into a source of oxygen. All the activities outlined above enrich life without causing pollution, unlike industry. The cinema makes it easier to decentralize entertainment. And if television were eventually to be completely free from government interference it could be a permanent source of education and could help to revive local culture. In France, for instance, if television were decentralized the people of Alsace, Britanny, the Basque country, Corsica and Provence could have their own programmes in their own language, which would no longer be looked down on. After all the Flemish population have managed it in Belgium.

How are we to set about slowing down the breakneck process of urbanization that's going on at the moment? The first step will be to apply economic pressure by raising taxes to a level where house-buying will become much more expensive, and by subsidizing building work on specially recommended sites. This would immediately cut down property speculation, which would subsequently be stopped altogether (because land would be collectivized) – plenty of gnashing of teeth there! But the most important step would be to create more jobs in country districts and small towns and fewer in large built-up areas.

If university campuses were made up of a large complex of teaching units and research units, colleges providing higher education etc., all covering a wide number of subjects, they could create stimulating centres of cultural and intellectual development in the heart of the countryside. In 1973 I had been struggling for exactly 40 years to teach (and learn!) the basic concepts of agriculture, and subsequently of husbandry and even 'development', at no. 16 rue Claude Bernard,* amid the paving-stones, the cement, the asphalt and the stink of petrol in the Latin Quarter in Paris! In 1976 we'll be celebrating the centenary of the date when it was built in the heart of Paris!

In giving people incentives to live in the country we shouldn't allow too much space to be taken up with private gardens and pleasure-grounds. If, as seems only too likely, our recommendations for halting the birth-rate aren't put into effect as quickly as seems desirable, and indeed essential, we probably have to earmark most of the land still available for farming and for communal leisure activities. For instance, the large grounds round stately homes in England would be open to the public, at least during certain fixed hours during a transitional period. In densely populated countries such as the Netherlands high-rise housing is essential if they want to preserve at any rate a minimum of agricultural land in the twenty-first century. Agriculture could in turn be reorganized along completely new lines. What does the future hold for today's fields?

### 9   *Everyone must be able to eat properly*

The poor countries can't get enough proteins. The communist countries – with the exception of China and her neighbours – are finding it very difficult to develop, modernize and intensify

* The address of the French Institut National Agronomique (*translator's note*).

their agriculture, except by increasing mechanization without proper planning. The rich countries can't find enough outlets for their products and are freezing an increasing proportion of their productive capacity, or destroying some of their products; they tend to be over-hasty in labelling goods as surpluses simply because they can't immediately find the necessary demand from people who can afford them. Peaches and pears that are allegedly unmarketable are deliberately spoiled, while in fact large numbers of children and old people living on low incomes would be delighted to eat them. Under today's economic system it is proving difficult to distribute them and yet ensure that the various activities involved remain economically viable. Which is another good reason for trying to change the system, to escape from it, either by means of violence or by a series of stages.

The total unsatisfied demand throughout the world is far higher than all our 'butter mountains' and other stocks. A system of distribution organized on a world scale would therefore be designed to encourage consumption of all produce by distributing all available purchasing power over a wide sector of the public, both on the national and international level. The first step in the transition to a socialist society and to survival would be to set up an international fund to buy up agricultural surpluses (starting with the produce that could provide proteins for children that I referred to earlier). They would then be distributed by the same fund to all those who needed them, not necessarily free of charge, since the cost to the consumer would depend on his personal resources.

In a study in the French edition of the FAO's *Nutrition Newsletter* (October/November 1971) Patrick François shows how if we relied solely on economic expansion to cut down malnutrition we should have to step up production to an impossible level – by a factor of 6 from 1962 to 1985:

> A monetary aid policy or a policy of distributing food to the groups of people in need is undoubtedly the most economical solution . . . a policy of safeguarding could be ensured by gifts from outside, in so far as they would not interfere with internal production by offering competition that is unacceptable in terms of economic development . . . A policy of increasing the amount of food available would be largely inoperative without a wide range of safeguarding measures on the economic and social levels.

Providing that this type of distribution didn't slow down

117

local agricultural output, which is what happens only too often with the notorious Public Law 480, which was basically designed to get rid of surpluses in North America (since widespread destruction of produce could look bad when the world is full of people starving to death), and to create a nice bit of propaganda for the United States in the process. This international fund would concentrate its efforts in three main areas. The first would be the parts of the world where famine is raging, as in Bangladesh in 1971–3. In August 1972 the Maulana Bashani said that thousands of his compatriots were starving to death, while the rest of the world remained indifferent to their plight. Chronic famine is the lot of poor families in India (admittedly famine has been raging there for thousands of years, but surely that doesn't make it any better?); as it has been for at least a hundred years in the Andes Mountains. Which only goes to show that international solidarity, the 'freedom from want' proclaimed when the United Nations was first set up, remains more or less a dead letter.

Pregnant women and nursing mothers and children up to the age of about 10 would be given special allowances. Distribution would be supervised to make sure that these sectors of the population, who have been shown (ever since the old League of Nations carried out its first investigations in 1937) to be more vulnerable when malnutrition is severe, really do get the minimum amount of proteins that are essential if their mental and physical capacities are ever to develop properly. It's no good thinking that school meals will do the trick, for at least two reasons: firstly, the poorest children and those who live furthest from school don't have them in many of the countries in southern Asia, Africa and even Central South America and the Middle East; secondly, even those who do have them are highly likely to have had their metabolisms irreparably damaged by nutritional deficiencies before they start school.

10  *Work-camps and agricultural reform*

The third set of operations would involve work-camps designed to feed peasant communities while they put in time improving the land during the slack season for agriculture, particularly when there's been a bad harvest. This would both increase the number of permanent jobs available and raise current figures for agricultural output. All over the world there are tremendous opportunities for investing labour in this type of work, starting with small-scale irrigation engineering, draining, protective measures against flooding and erosion, planting fruit-trees and forests, levelling paddy fields so that high-yield varieties of rice can be grown, fencing off land and creating ley-farming pastures, building access strips etc.

In my earlier books I showed the extent to which this type of work is neglected, particularly in India, where it is often neglected in favour of housing and making villages accessible to the outside world, both of which, although useful, are much less urgent. We must work out an order of priorities, giving preference to anything liable to increase output and the number of jobs available. It is better to stave off the possibility of famine by feeding those who work in these work-camps, than to be compelled to rescue them at some later date by means of soup-kitchens. Soup-kitchens are not only unproductive, they are an affront to the dignity of those who are fed by them. Our aim must be to offer work, not to encourage begging.

The results produced by this type of work-camp are not always as good as in China. In India *shramdan,* voluntary labour, has dropped to a very low level almost everywhere, to almost nothing – a real farce! In Tunisia many peasants left their fields in about 1956–60 and fled to camps set up for the unemployed, where they could earn more than by farming their very poor land. The work-camps concentrated chiefly on anti-erosion measures, but often on land that wasn't worth the work involved. They also organized planting on land that was never properly marked out, with the result that no one bothered to look after it subsequently. The overall results were pretty poor, because red tape had a stranglehold on all these activities.[9]

The 'national promotion' scheme in Morocco included planting vines for producing grapes in the Riff, but as the peasants were working on land that didn't belong to them they didn't bother about it unduly and concentrated on making the project last as long as possible – they were interested in the extra money, not in the results of their work.

In the end it was increasingly the generals and other top people who benefited from it in recent years. In 1971 only 1 or 2 per cent of the days worked in the Azrou area were devoted to work for the public good, such as irrigation or anti-erosion measures. The rest went on private properties, and the officers made their men work there as well. Similarly, the citrus-fruit plantations on the state-run farms in Cuba haven't always been looked after properly – you've only got to see how slowly the trees have grown . . . .

The least expensive form of work, both for the national community and for the world community, is work done by peasants in their own villages or in the immediate neighbourhood, since this saves the whole cost of clothing, transport and even hand-tools for the paramilitary youth-battalions. They will do their best work, particularly as far as planting is concerned, if they are working for themselves on their own farms instead of for the local landowner, tradesman or money-lender, or on a collective farm run on bureaucratic lines, unless they have *volunteered* to join it. This raises the preliminary question of agricultural reform which, although vitally necessary, has often produced extremely poor results, or has even made things worse. In underdeveloped areas a system whereby peasants farm their own land will probably continue for many decades yet to be the best solution. We must therefore help them by setting up various types of community groups.

If the peasants are given a minimum of general, technical and financial training it will be easier to make them understand at some point in the future that once a certain stage of development has been reached, as it has in Chile or Cuba, the *microfundium* can no longer be modernized economically. Along with Jacques Chonchol in Chile we would therefore give priority to educating these peasants, and later to giving them permanent training by means of a body of trained staff who would impart knowledge more by persuasion than by authoritarian teaching and would therefore have to be completely devoted to the peasant cause, i.e. politically motivated. At this point small collective farms would have a better chance of success than huge state-run farms, providing the peasants actually asked for them and were allowed to run them themselves. People working in small teams of this kind would be less likely to shirk, because they'd know that they were stealing from their own workmates whom they knew personally . . . . It would also be important to make sure that the State didn't allow large industrial and commercial firms to exploit semi-skilled outfits of this kind. If they did, as Michel Gutelman so felicitously put it, agrarian reform would soon turn into agrarian mystification.[10] We should therefore soon have to set up a system for organizing supplies and marketing outlets for these peasants and small collective farms, on a more centralized basis this time, so that they could sell their produce more easily on the national or international markets.

The exact details of this type of scheme, which has been written with the *latifundia* of South America in mind, could not be worked out until we knew which country we were talking about and the stage of development it had reached. For instance the right solution for Zambia, where we're starting off with what is known as a 'primitive' nomadic culture and it seems advisable to retain a peasant community, would be quite different from the system appropriate for Chile or Argentina, once the necessary 'reforms' have been carried out and a large estate has been divided up. Up to now studies of ways of making the transition to various forms of socialism have ignored these agrarian problems, or oversimplified them. The issue of survival will raise a whole lot of other questions.

11   *A system of agriculture geared to quality produce and survival, but for a limited world population*

It seems to me that ecologists are being a bit over-hasty in condemning modern agricultural methods wholesale by talking about our fields under cultivation as 'artificial monocultures'. Admittedly it would be useful to examine more closely the question of polycultures that involve clearing land, the type of thing practised by nomadic farming communities, who are too easily dismissed as 'primitive'. The figures for the yield of yams grown on cleared forest land on the northern coast of New Guinea are impressive. Attempts to encourage the Africans to switch to monocultures, particularly cotton, have been somewhat precipitate, because the whole question has never been gone into properly – which is what we must do now.

I have already rejected the idea that all forms of chemical fertilizers are automatically to be condemned wholesale, which is what those who advocate 'biological agriculture' would have us think, since they state dogmatically, though they haven't yet produced any evidence for this, that all these 'chemical' fertilizers are harmful. Everything in nature is made up of a number of constituents that can be described in terms of chemical elements – so there's no reason why the word 'chemical' should be thought of as pejorative. Having said that, there's an urgent case for stopping farmers using too much fertilizer, and the ecologists deserve credit for speaking out against this practice.

The finest example, if I may be allowed to put it like that, of dangerous 'modernist' extravagance is the one I gave in Part I, Section 8, where I referred to the waste matter that is casually dumped in rivers in the United States, along with huge over-doses of nitrates, which are then harmful. We must encourage everybody to use their organic refuse sensibly, whether they've got a farm or just a vegetable-garden or even an ordinary flower garden; as we've seen, in 1936–44 the Germans used to put theirs in a separate container so that it could be used for pigfeed. At any rate let's keep it for manure, which will improve the soil structure, reduce erosion and cut down the need for artificial fertilizers. If our sewers took organic waste straight to the fields they would fertilize the soil and pollute the water less. If we ploughed up more grazing-land we could cut down the use of nitrates with leguminous plants.

In May 1972 I noticed that one Saturday the city of Melbourne was covered with clouds of smoke. I discovered that all the people living in the suburbs, which means most of the population in Melbourne, were burning the autumn leaves from their gardens in incinerators, instead of turning them into compost! The North Vietnamese leave their night-soil to ferment at a temperature high enough to kill any germs, and then use it as fertilizer. At any rate it can be buried instead of being spread over market-gardens. Our direct-to-sewer drainage system must be revised and all this fermentable refuse must be taken straight to the fields.

Insects can be controlled by the use of non-toxic insecticides of vegetable origin, such as pyrethrum. Or with insects, viruses or other organisms that live off the ones that do the damage. The introduction of herbicides or tractors in countries where there is a high level of unemployment is a highly debatable question, as I recently had occasion to point out in relation to Ceylon, in particularly dramatic circumstances.[11] The funds allocated for research into these biological techniques of insect-prevention are nowhere near large enough, since non-polluting methods of this kind are often harder to get just right.

The way we look at agriculture in the future will depend in essence on the number of mouths we've got to feed. Today's 'North Atlantic' type of diet represents a luxury way of feeding people, and at the moment it is in fact exclusive to the rich nations. There is no chance of being able to distribute comparable quantities of beef and other produce from stockbreeding to the world population of 7 thousand million that is forecast for the year 2000, even if we managed to fulfil the most ridiculously optimistic forecasts for growth in agricultural output.

An increasingly spartan diet would thus have to be implemented as the size of the population increased. In particular this would involve a vegetarian diet, with proteins extracted from leaves, oil-cakes, algae, yeast from oil and other microorganisms. The poor in Iran are too proud to accept such food, 'because it comes from the rich'. All this would give a sensible and balanced diet, and a reasonably palatable one. Fruit, which is often cheaper than vegetables, would be used as a substitute for them in some instances.

As for those who would like to think that their great-grandchildren will be able to get hold of camembert, a nice piece of beef or a dish of seafood they'll simply have to realize that this will depend on the decisions they themselves take about birth-control in the next few years. A rich diet with oysters and vintage wines and champagne can only ever be available for a limited number of people. The only way to achieve this limited number is either to cut down the overall population, or to increase the present level of injustice by adopting a system of global apartheid by which ores would be reserved exclusively for the rich and the majority of the human race would continue to exist at a subhuman level. Slavery hasn't yet been entirely wiped out in places ranging from India and Ceylon (Sri Lanka) to Mauritania, and in many other places besides. In the West it takes the form of immigrant labour. In the tropics they're called peasants, *fellahin, nhaqués, conucos, métayers (bargardars), raiyats* etc.

Lastly, a system of agriculture geared to survival would be designed to protect the common heritage of mankind, our land, from all forms of destruction. This will involve firstly giving it a dressing of humus, then adopting various techniques designed to conserve the soil, the first aim being to prevent various forms of erosion. Certain types of animal energy might be used here. Once you've shaken off the idea of trying to make more money and are no longer rushed off your feet and worn out, working with horses, oxen or mules can be very pleasant. 'It gives you a chance to sort your ideas out,' as Jules Grand, a market-gardener in Cavaillon, used to tell me. It would be even more pleasant if you were working at sea.

12    *The seas are not inexhaustible, so they must become public property*

The FAO thinks that one day it may *perhaps* be possible to raise the figure of 69 million metric tons of fish caught at sea in 1972 to 140 million metric tons. But this figure could not be achieved without considerable difficulty and we couldn't go above it without cutting into existing stocks, and thus cutting down future yields. This has already happened in the case of whaling and sardine-fishing in California, and it is happening now in the case of Atlantic salmon and North Sea herrings, though these are not the only examples. Admittedly the current output of living organisms from the sea is of the order of 100 thousand million metric tons, but phytoplankton and zooplankton, those microscopic organisms that were said to be in inexhaustible supply, 'cannot be economically fished in the foreseeable future'.

Then again these forecasts include 20 million metric tons from inland fishing-grounds – rivers, lakes and reservoirs, or ponds specially reserved for fish-farming – and the future of such fishing-grounds depends largely on the level of pollution in the years to come. There are plans for developing fish-farming at sea, which at the moment applies chiefly to molluscs and to a certain extent to algae, but which could be expanded to include fish as well, particularly in estuaries and coastal lagoons where conditions are very favourable. But the problem is that it's these coastal areas and low-lying valleys that face the biggest threat from increasing pollution. They would be used chiefly for oysters and other shellfish, all of which are luxury foods. Only mussels can offer an economic source of nutrition, and they are useful for the poor countries because they require comparatively little work.

Some marshes that are difficult to drain or unsuitable for fish-breeding – because they're too acid, with toxic 'free' aluminium salts – and are therefore being converted at vast expense into poor paddy-fields would be much better suited to intensive fish-farming. They could be turned into ponds that would produce much more food, especially protein. The plans drawn up for the development of rice-growing in Taiwan and Korea are being looked at again in the light of this, and in the future, once peace has returned, it could affect some of the 'toxic' paddy-fields in South Vietnam, which have been causing too much trouble to the local peasants and the agronomists.

But according to a message from Bertrand de Jouvenel in *Pacem in Maribus* (1971) the seas are no longer 'a liquid mass bearing ships and containing fish . . . it rests on rich deposits of oil and natural gas'. As a result the Americans, who have squandered so many of their natural resources and are beginning to worry about running out of oil, on which they've based their whole development, indeed their whole civilization, announced on 28 September, 1945 that the natural resources of the soil and subsoil of the continental shelf that projects into the high seas from the coasts of the United States came under their control and were under their jurisdiction. This 'shelf' was defined as having a depth of water of less than 200 metres, which gave the United States, at a single stroke, 'control' over more than 2 million square kilometres of ocean, more than 4 times the area of France!

This means that they're hardly entitled to contest, as they are at the moment, the proclamation made by Chile, Ecuador and Peru on 18 August, 1952 in Santiago that they were going to extend their sovereignty and jurisdiction over a maritime zone of 370 kilometres beyond their coastline, even if the continental shelf is much narrower on the Pacific coast. The United States' main concern was oil. And in fact a growing proportion of hydrocarbon is being extracted from the seabed every year. The figure is apparently already 15 per cent, and over 40 per cent is forecast for 1980; but there's a growing danger of pollution and the safety measures that are being taken are totally inadequate. The dangers increase when the oil is transported by sea; and this now represents over half of all sea transport, and 62 per cent of the tons/kilometres that have been extracted!

The vast size of the tankers also increases the danger, since they now have a capacity of over ½ million metric tons. And so does the inadequacy of the safety measures taken under cover of flags of convenience, such as the Liberian flag under which the notorious *Torrey Canyon* sailed. Its captain had been on duty for 336 days without a break, so it's not surprising it hit a reef near the Scilly Isles at the far western tip of Great Britain.

The daily running costs of these monster-tankers are so high that they must be constantly on the move if they're to continue to make a profit – but they could have relieved the crew! If we allow the present state of virtual *laissez-faire* to continue and do not enforce rules that haven't got enough teeth anyway, the waste matter discharged into the sea from rivers and sewers, plus the refuse thrown overboard from ships, and most of all the huge quantities of pollutant material that are dumped when the petrol-tankers clean up at sea, are going to cut output and make the high seas, the last open spaces on the globe, far less pleasant. The 'floating palaces' I'm going to recommend are very different from Colin Clark's (Part I, section 1).

At the present moment huge numbers of people throughout the world are unemployed. A never-failing supply of wind blows across the sea. The trade winds used to be used for crossing the Atlantic and the monsoon blows at intervals over the Indian Ocean. Many young people would like to study oceanography or simply to breathe the invigorating sea air and sometimes battle against storms. What is today a luxury for sport-loving millionaires could become, in view of the imminent shortages of fuel (which will be restricted to the petrochemical industry), a constructive activity and at the same time a delightful pastime. These young people would build sailing-ships ranging from 1,000 metric tons for coasters to 20,000 metric tons for new transatlantic liners, which would always take advantage of the most favourable winds, information on this being supplied by radio by the Meteorological Offices, together with further recommendations worked out by computer. In suggesting these sailing-ships, I am assuming that we shall have been successful in cutting down the population, since otherwise all our Utopian schemes would come to nothing.

But the seas also represent the only open space on the planet that has never been nationalized. It's now high time we *inter*nationalized them fully. In other words, they should be placed under a communal authority whose first task would be to put a stop to all those terrifying arms that Robin Clarke tells us are lurking on the high seas. It would then draw up rules for fishing, so as to protect existing species and thus future food production. But most important of all, if the seabed, which holds out such high hopes with its metals as well as its oil, became public property it would be worked on behalf of the whole international community, especially those members that need it most. Thus the backward and dominated countries would receive royalties, or better still would themselves help to extract these riches from the sea.

These communal open spaces are rapidly shrinking. Now the coastal areas that the various nations are beginning to appropriate are far and away the most interesting, both because they contain more plentiful supplies of fish and because the seabed is more accessible there. It would have been better if they'd been declared international when the United Nations was founded in 1945, before the Truman Declaration mentioned above. But in that case we would have needed a genuinely international authority that people could respect. If we want to lengthen the life of our planet we'll have to organize this one day, preferably in the very near future. But how do we set about it?

Now that I've sketched out some of the economic measures that I feel should be given priority both in the backward and dominated countries and in the rich countries and at sea, I must take a closer look – though not too close – at the political problems that these measures will inevitably give rise to. As they will be linked to the extent to which people are aware of the situation at each stage, they will force us to rethink our whole concept of education, as Ivan Illich recommends.

Before this happens I'm going once again to give free rein to my indignation, which represents the first stage of revolt – even if I get accused of preaching or of being sentimental. My reason for remaining faithful to the values implicit in socialism is that I have a deep-seated feeling that I simply cannot accept the most blatant injustices, not that I've got a preconceived view of the meaning of history. I didn't object when a communist journal described me as a 'sentimental' socialist. If socialists don't have a better-developed sense of social justice how can they justify their existence? After all, socialism's got off to a bad start only too often.

The United States is short of petrol, the demand for beef is exceeding supplies, the reserves of cereals are melting away and India and Bangladesh can't get enough to feed all their people. All these warning signals have flashed on at the same moment, yet the people at the top are like shortsighted drivers who refuse to wear glasses. It's high time we grabbed the driving-wheel from them, before a collision takes away our last hope of survival. The time has gone when we could squabble about the exact meaning of some text written by Lenin or Rosa Luxemburg.

The FAO has issued a solemn warning: millions of people from Dakar to Dacca are going to starve to death. India couldn't buy the 6 million metric tons of cereals she needs and the 3 she has bought have completely cleaned her out, since she had to pay much more for them. Bangladesh will be $1\frac{1}{2}$ million metric tons short, even if we take into account the 'normal' situation of only one meal per day for 3 months of the year. In 1966 I called one of my books *The Hungry Future*. I'm very sorry indeed to see that my fears were justified (cf. *Ouest-France,* 20 February, 1973).

## Part V

## INJUSTICE OR SURVIVAL? NEW MEN AND NEW POWERS

1 *Dominance, armaments, exploitation, alienation, waste – we've had enough of all that!*

Two facts remain: we are trying to build up
some relatively rational Utopias, though they are by definition
premature; and the world is not governed by Reason alone.
Yet we must act quickly, because the dangers are imminent
and we are all hostages to survival. Even before we have
exhausted our non-renewable resources and pollution has
reached an intolerable level our world, with its many injustices, is capable of escalating the poverty and the revolts
and making them increase faster. Revolts are already breaking
out at various points on the globe, so they're no longer purely
hypothetical.

The Club of Rome is urging us to put an end to growth.
That's all very well, but this extremely relative 'end' would be
acceptably only if a whole series of preliminary steps had been
taken. I shall now have another go at outlining these pre-
liminaries and sorting them into groups, the idea being to try
to give those of our young people who refuse to opt out new
reasons for fighting and a few glimmers of hope.

I shall start by recommending that the influential people in
the rich countries, plus their allies within the privileged
minorities in the dominated countries, should bring their
dominance over the people and working populations of the
poor countries to an end. In a recent issue of *Le Monde* Tibor
Mende advised that we should:

> ... tackle the undeniable conflict of interest between on the one
> hand an industrialized world that is determined to keep and
> increase its opulence, and on the other the people who live in the

129

under-developed countries, who are struggling to survive and to retain their dignity ... the industrial world brings together the interests and cultural preferences of the governing minorities in the countries receiving aid ... cutting down rather than improving the poor countries' ability to import productive materials, and maintaining in power minorities whose policies involve continuing to implement methods that are much more expensive than all the aid they receive.[1]

If we are 'at least to stop doing harm', he recommends that we should put a stop to arms-buying, the brain-drain, the flight of capital (belonging to the rich and to the leaders) and turning a blind eye to corruption. At first glance it looks as though we could do this without reforming the whole structure, simply by implementing a policy of 'honest capitalism' – though you only have to put the two words side by side to realize how ill-matched they are.

The main clash today is no longer between employers and employees, between government and governed in the rich countries. In New York I saw a gang of construction workers setting off to fight the students of the University of Columbia, who were protesting against the Vietnam War. And in 1972 these 'members of the proletariat' preferred Nixon to McGovern! It seems to me that the major clash today is an insidious one between on the one hand the proletariat of the modern era – which means the vast rural communities – plus those who live in shanty-towns, and those who are out of work or underemployed and living in great poverty in the dominated countries, and on the other *all* those who exploit them, including the highly paid workers in the rich countries, driving round in their big cars in Toronto or New York, Chicago or Los Angeles – and in Paris. A hundred years ago Engels was stressing the fact that English workers were taking advantage of British imperialism. The ambiguous position of our working class in western Europe prevents them from fighting with all their strength against worldwide injustices, because they too are taking advantage of them.

An even more urgent need, though it may seem even more difficult to achieve – in fact the two are linked – is to put a stop to the arms race, which is wasting scarce resources, bringing nearer the day when there'll be appalling shortages, ruining the poor countries and threatening all of us with a slow genetic deterioration and with the likelihood of bringing the world to a sudden death by nuclear suicide. One day the supranational powers that are a feature of my Utopian schemes – if they don't come too late, that is – would have sole control over the power that would still be necessary if their arbitration were to carry any weight.

Since South Africa and even Israel can afford to cock a snook at the United Nations, and the United States have got away with destroying people, towns and schools, dykes, flora and fauna in Vietnam without being arraigned before the civilized nations, a world policing body couldn't be set up unless the nations who are most directly concerned insisted on it, or in other words until they seized power themselves. Don't forget that during at least three springs (Paris in 1936 and 1968 and Prague in 1968) the mass of ordinary people managed to go further than the political parties, and forced them to go further than they'd ever gone before. But they didn't take over the reins of power, not anywhere.

We must aim for an end to exploitation and a feeling of alienation by trying to build up by gradual stages, not an ideal, angelic and perfect society, but one that is fairer and less wasteful and involves fewer constraints. Our goal most be to create a variety of forms of socialism (though we shall never be able to realize all possible forms) that are more concerned with long-term survival than the present regimes. Interesting experiments along these lines are being conducted in countries as far apart as Chile and Tanzania, China and Yugoslavia or Vietnam, plus the 'international protest movement', and not forgetting Peking in 1966. We've been so badly led astray that we're stuck in a tunnel, and we've got a long way to go yet before we see the light at the end of it. At any rate concepts such as exploitation and alienation will always give rise to arguments and will remain open questions; even the concept of 'excessive profit' is difficult to define and calculate in concrete terms.

We must also put an end to waste, in all its forms – and it takes many forms – by going back to the grass roots of the peasant ethic, which is based on austerity, providence, prudence and great dignity. Having lived through two world wars I've been compelled to work to produce more (1914–18) and to provide transport (1940–4). As a result I'm still so shocked by the slightest form of waste that my young friends, particularly those in Quebec, are quite amazed. It's not for nothing that I was brought up with an almost religious respect for bread – which only goes to show how much your upbringing can influence you. Since the people available to build our new societies are far from perfect, the only way to prevent the privileged few, even if their privileges are fairly modest, from going on wasting in the same slap-happy fashion as today, and with impunity, is to make sure that incomes are distributed much more fairly.

Our first target must be all those endless and frequently pointless car trips, since they represent the most important and the best symbol for all the other forms of waste. According to Marc Penouil,[2] General Motors' budget is the equivalent of 6 times the total combined GNP of the seven states of the West African Economic Community (which was set up by a treaty signed in Bamako on 3 June 1970), i.e. the Ivory Coast, Dahomey, the Upper Volta, Mali, Mauritania, Niger and Senegal! The GNP of the richest of the seven states, the Ivory Coast, which was calculated as 1.4 thousand million dollars in 1969, was the same as the gross product of the Renault company! We take waste for granted, since it is an indispensable factor in a profit economy. But we could be educated – or re-educated – to get no pleasure at all from commodities that harm the most underprivileged sectors. After all the great majority of our private cars are merely a symbol of the way the privileged few take advantage of their position, to such an intolerable extent that they actually help to make the poor poorer, and to endanger our survival.

2 *Revolt, overcrowding and real austerity, or fewer people living in comfort?*

Finally, and this is the most important part, we must stop the population explosion, or otherwise our whole Utopia will never get off the ground. As the rich and improvident nations grow bigger, the time when widespread shortages and an unbearable level of pollution will be the order of the day looms closer and closer. At the same time we must stop an increase in the population of the poor countries that are already overpopulated, which means the Caribbean and the Andes, Egypt and particularly southern Asia. Even assuming that we will gradually manage to distribute people and particularly goods more evenly over the globe, rather as I have advocated above, we shall have to choose between large numbers of people and affluence. In the first case increasingly harsh austerity and all the privations that entails; in the second case a world population figure restricted to a level at which *everyone* would be assured of a life worth living, and at which we could conserve nature and thus guarantee the survival of the species.

Admittedly, as Tibor Mende puts it, the rich countries will be able to try to hide 'mounting tension and widespread poverty behind the repressive veil of a sort of worldwide system of apartheid', while at the same time keeping the ore and the oil for themselves. But in that case revolts would break out all over the place. So we have a choice between (a) a world characterized by injustices and growing revolt, leading to a worldwide catastrophe that is bound to happen if we allow present trends to continue; or (b) the discipline – which will become increasingly harsh – of a world that is more egalitarian but is overcrowded and thus repressive all over again, a world in which travel in particular will be strictly rationed; or (c) a comfortable life (which incidentally could be extremely pleasant for all those who enjoy the simple things of life, nature, the arts and real communication with their fellow-men) for a limited number of people; the numbers would have to be kept as low as possible if we want to enjoy it.

In 1975 the world population will be nearly 4 thousand million, which seems to me too high. If we want to achieve a very high standard of living and allow it to continue indefinitely we must cut down this figure very considerably, by at least half. Anyone who is resigned to a figure of 7 thousand million in the year 2000 really hasn't grasped the manifold consequences of allowing irresponsible people to 'breed like rabbits'. If we are going to double our population in 30 years it is essential that we should build up or organize over that period the same amount of housing, the same potential for agricultural and industrial output, the same facilities for education and medicine, even the same number of roads, railways, canals and other means of communication, and the same number of hospitals, schools etc. as over the thousands of years of civilization that came before us.

To say 'the same' is in fact inaccurate, if we really want to lessen injustice by raising very considerably the subhuman standard of living experienced by the majority of the human race, once the most dangerous forms of waste have been cut back. We would have to 'do' much more than the sum total of what has been achieved since the time of the pharaohs. I've looked in vain in the forecasts published in the United States or by the United Nations for some sign that the difficulties of the task before us are fully appreciated – with the exception of the one issued by the International Labour Organization in October 1972. Learned calculations to see what the future will bring won't do any more. The house is on fire and the time has come to send for the fire brigade. Medical research can invent even more effective and convenient methods of contraception, and the rich countries could make these available to the poorest countries (once they'd made sure that their own people were using them extensively).

But before the people concerned will allow us to put forward this kind of policy we must first educate them and we must also adopt a series of measures to bring about genuine solidarity right across this planet on which we're all marooned, whether we like it or not. In other words, we must first seize power from the rich and powerful. Over the next few years they will no doubt stoop to using threats and even war – as in Vietnam – to ensure that they can go on wasting as many scarce raw materials as they do now – the figure is already exorbitant – or even more. It's the rape of the Third World all over again.

In 1951 President Truman asked Philip H. Coombs to prepare a report on supplies of raw materials down to 1975. Somewhat oddly, this was given the title 'Resources for Freedom' (incidentally the Quebec branch of the FLQ worked out a plan to blow off the arm carrying the lamp on the Statue of Liberty at the entrance to New York Harbour, but they never made it). One day the Chinese will be entitled to put in a claim for the share of the world's scarce resources that they're saving now by accepting a degree of austerity.

So far I have basically suggested that when young people get together they should chant a series of slogans, of incantations rather like the endless litanies that parish priests used to make their pious elderly female parishioners chant in church. Now in spite of all these litanies no one has ever managed to create a world inspired by the Gospels. We are faced once again with *the* one fundamental problem, the problem of Power with a capital P. Here again I am neither over-optimistic nor over-pessimistic. Everything will depend on the speed with which the majority of the exploited nations become fully and deeply aware of the gravity of the situation, and manage to grasp where it is going to lead them . . . .

### 3 *Catastrophes are probably inevitable*

The forces of anti-imperialism are still too weak and, more important, too divided among themselves to hope for a quick killing. It would be reasonable to hesitate before including the Soviet Union under this heading, since although she gives aid to Vietnam her army has occupied Czechoslovakia and she too 'dominates' one region – the whole of Eastern Europe. Within the Soviet Union itself Roy Medvedev's book on Stalinism[3] shows us a society that is still largely infected by the totalitarian poison. It is therefore highly likely that the dominated countries will continue to be dominated for a long time to come, particularly as they are so divided among themselves – a fact that the UNCTAD conference in Santiago in April/May 1972 couldn't conceal. According to people at the FAO, the delegates they send to the international organizations haven't always got enough technical knowledge to defend their case properly.

At this point in my argument the pen is liable to drop from my fingers. At the very end of the nineteenth century the peasants in the Charente district of France refused to set up collective dairies until they'd really been through the mill for several years, because of the way they were exploited by the butter trade. The rich and powerful of this world, and even we semi-privileged people, will not grasp the danger in the way things are going at the present moment until they themselves are affected personally and seriously by the situation. But by then pollution will have become intolerable and metal-ores will be very scarce. And the poor will no longer put up with a level of poverty that is an affront to their dignity when they compare it to the opulence of the rich, which is increasing all the time.

It will clearly be much more difficult to put things right and a harsh degree of austerity will have to be imposed if we put it off to a later stage. If we don't start controlling births until later we'll have to be much tougher about it if we're to survive at all. My only consolation will perhaps be the thought that unless I am much mistaken I sounded the warning in time, along with many other people. But we won't be there to see for ourselves. Even if many people feel that the Club of Rome are being too pessimistic, I reckon that they owe it to themselves to be over-pessimistic if they're in any doubt. We can't go on gambling on the survival of mankind by placing a long series of wagers that are considerably more idiotic and dangerous than Pascal's.

So our only hope is that the great majority of people will become aware in the very near future of the extremely grave situation in which we find ourselves. Barry Commoner has shown that if water pollution becomes so serious that the surface has to go increasingly short of oxygen, quite apart from the foetid smell that will be noticeable everywhere, the dangerous bacteria that proliferate in the soil will develop there, increasing the danger of epidemics to an alarming extent. We simply don't know where we're going any more. As well as the well-founded anxieties expressed by the Club of Rome we must add a concern for genuine social justice both nationally and, even more, internationally (and this concern must be expressed more forcefully than their timid appeal). This would be the only way to disarm potential terrorists representing the world's poor – for tomorrow they won't just be Palestinians if we dare to go on exploiting as much as we are now, or even more.

The only hope for these people in their wretchedness, as they're beginning to realize increasingly clearly, will be to frighten us. And because our society is ultra-complex and ultra-artificial, it is becoming increasingly vulnerable to daring attacks by people who won't hesitate to sacrifice their own lives in the process. Well, then? We must try to rebuild a genuine New World (I daren't go on using the term New Society, since that's become such a dirty word by now) on foundations that have been entirely rethought, with people trained, forged and reforged by completely new methods of education within a framework of social structures that are constantly evolving.

4    *We must stamp out contempt for manual
     labour by bringing the production process into
     the schoolroom*

The segregation between manual workers and intellectuals
that operates today, sometimes to a more marked extent than
ever, leads many young people from well-off families to move
from school to university without ever doing any real work
at all up to the age of 25, or even 27! Later on, as they step
straight from their car into their office or their home, they
will never turn their hand to any manual work, except possibly
mowing the lawn or the odd day's sport. Meanwhile what
remains of the proletariat is no longer large enough to collect
our rubbish and sweep our streets and be our domestic
servants. So we have to turn to a new class of slaves, known
as 'immigrants', who have come, in the case of France, from
Spain and Portugal, the Maghreb and more recently tropical
Africa. My stonemason in Aix introduces his Tunisian
labourer as his 'slave', and treats him accordingly. The
differential between the rates of pay for different kinds of work
is widening in the West, rather than narrowing, and on the
international scale it's widening even further.

The contempt for manual work instilled by this system of
education soon spreads to the man doing the manual work,
particularly if there's an element of racialism in it. As long as
it continues, any attempt to create a fairer society will never
get beyond the stage of an edifying proposal, an 'incantation'.
Even the Soviet Union hasn't managed to wipe out this
feeling of contempt entirely. First and foremost it is essential
that everyone should have done a fair amount of manual work,
at least when he's young. There's no question of going back
to the bad old days of child labour in 1820–40, but I've always
been delighted to see American boys doing a paper round
after school to earn their own pocket-money, students in
Quebec earning most of the fees for their 7 months' of study
during the remaining 5 months of vacation. When my
students at Ottawa University were working alongside
agricultural labourers they had a good deal to tell me, I can
tell you!

In China the village school includes a garden in which
children start working at a very early age. Six-year-olds can
thin out seedlings, weed, as long as the earth isn't too heavy,

water plants with a small watering-can and start growing their own vegetables. If they've created their own little garden with the sweat of their brow they're less likely to lose interest in it. As well as showing respect for the work and the person who does it they'll also respect the results of such work. For 10-year-olds upwards Chinese schools set up workshops to make functional articles, which are then sold. So the children are actually involved in the production process. Instead of being parasites they are visibly very proud of helping to build a socialist society, even at that age.

In that kind of society work has become the most valuable thing of all, along with studying socialism. It is even pleasurable in itself, for wealth is no longer valued. As soon as society stops encouraging people to make money the idea of acquiring possessions no longer seems particularly attractive. People manage very nicely without a car in China or Vietnam. If the French had known how to foster a similar state of mind in schools in tropical Africa they would be less of a drain on the local exchequers, which can no longer maintain them, and, more important, they would produce fewer people who can't get work. What happens at the moment is that most of their pupils refuse to do any form of manual work, which their semi-educated brains think of as being solely for the illiterate. By using your hands, not on a soul-destroying assembly line on the factory floor but on a craftsman's workbench, you develop, alongside the manual inventiveness that is common to all children, a different type of intelligence, but one that is no less important than the ability to go in for abstract reasoning. Work that is varied and properly integrated, with shifts in the factory alternating with shifts on the land, is a real delight, according to William Morris, since the old dichotomies of manual/intellectual or urban/rural disappear.

This is where we must act quickly, by refusing to resign ourselves to the present situation. We must learn simply to *be*. The report prepared by the Edgar Faure Commission of UNESCO does not come out strongly enough against the harm done by westernized education systems in the dominated countries.. It has been predicted that in 1980, 230 million children aged between 5 and 14 will have no schooling at all, and that there will still be 820 million illiterate adults (29 per cent, though the figures for men and women are 40 and 20 per cent respectively). These forecasts don't mention those who are virtually illiterate, who have learnt nothing in the

1 to 3 years they spent in school. But the forecasts could in fact be largely reversed if we began right now to rethink our whole concept of education, giving priority to new campaigns for teaching reading and writing on a functional basis, followed by a continuous process of education along completely new lines, instead of the present school system, which is too expensive and pretty inefficient. The new scheme would go further than UNESCO, the initial aim being to make peasant communities understand the modern socio-economic and political world of today. Otherwise they will never be able to fit into the modern world and play their own part in it, which will be a decisive one.

Although the Faure Report was supposed to be international it unfortunately fails to mention what has been happening in China, though in fact Edgar Faure himself is familiar with developments there. This considerably lessens its value.

Agricultural output could be stepped up very considerably if the young people involved (peasants, craftsmen, labourers, all of whom are left out in the cold under the present education system) were given special technical and social training in modern techniques and modern social structures, as well as in reading and writing. Under my scheme most of the funds intended for education, which would now be treated as a continuous process, would be spent on this combination of teaching literacy and training. The classic school, which would be allocated less money, would make its pupils work. This would take care of most of their schooling fees. Once the peasants had learnt to read and write and undergone this form of training they would at last be able to have a hand in their own fate, to get a real grasp of the problems created by modernizing farming and commercialization . . . and by domination. In the new type of school they would begin to have a share in their children's education, as in China, and would later set up their own cooperative societies.

The main aim of the educational system would not be to bring up children on a selective élitist basis, concentrating on the tiny minority who go on to higher education almost to the exclusion of the others. Instead an attempt would be made to group everyone in the village – children, adolescents and adults – into a single collective pattern of education, which would be a continuous process in which everyone would learn from everyone else. Ivan Illich has roughed out some interesting schemes along these lines, but he didn't go far enough. The most difficult part will be how best to train the teachers, since they will have to be more than mere educators: they will have to be capable of putting over their material in a lively way and well-versed in politics. Ultimately they would have to be real apostles.

In Cuba a system of boarding schools linked to coffee, pineapple or citrus fruit plantations has been devised, so secondary education is again tied up with the production process. This seems to me the best solution. Once peasants were better educated they would be better at organizing themselves, and would be less willing to put up with the way their privileged minorities abuse the system. Power would start changing hands, particularly if all the progressive elements in the rich countries put their shoulder to the same wheel by giving up the unfair privileges they now enjoy. But when will they take in that their privileges are unfair?

Just as this scheme involving half-school and half-work seems best for the backward countries in the early stages, similar schemes could be implemented in the rich countries. But once these young people have been through this new type of school they won't become genuinely 'new men' until organized society no longer offers them the present spectacle of blatant inequalities. Our transition to socialism in the countries that are still rich might perhaps begin with a Swedish-style version of socialism, under which incomes are distributed on a fairer basis, providing that there was much greater concern than in Sweden (which is itself a privileged nation) about the economic power and ultimate fate of the oppressed countries.

Yet if we are to make the transition to a form of socialism we must first undergo a considerable political evolution. The problem is how to set about this. France today is far too imbued with the petit-bourgeois mentality and is thoroughly selfish. But the militants and the younger generation do represent a glimmer of hope that can no longer be overlooked, particularly since May 1968. Always providing they can shake off their moroseness and their feeling of boredom, and providing they aren't afraid to criticize adult society at every turn, at home as well as outside. Most of all, the most ardent of them must break away from the series of dogmatic attitudes that encourage in-fighting instead of a joint stand against the common enemy. A militant who does his 45 hours a week in a factory and then spends an additional 15 to 20 hours on unpaid union work, thus running the risk of losing his job (as at Citroën or Simca), is a sounder version of the 'new man' than a student can ever be.

## 5  A common left-wing platform for the Third World

If the militants and young people continue to be split up into large numbers of sects and chapels whose main concern is arguing about the interpretation of such and such a paragraph in the 'sacred' texts of Marx or Lenin, Trotsky or Mao, Rosa Luxemburg or Che Guevara – not to mention the greats of yesteryear (Fourier, Saint-Simon, Proudhon etc.) – they'll never get anything much done. Yet we've seen that they are capable of presenting a united front when the cause is sufficiently uplifting, as with Vietnam's fight against US imperialism. But now that the war is pretty well over this shouldn't weaken the idea of a common front on behalf of the condemned people of this earth, the most exploited people on the whole planet. The battle isn't over yet, and it may never be over, according to Mao Tse-tung.

The battle against the economic and political domination of the under-industrialized countries by the 'central capitalism' of the rich countries could bring about a platform of united action, though this has yet to be worked out. It would have the dual aim of less inequality and improved chances of survival, and would operate on a worldwide scale, leaving doctrinal problems aside for the time being. This united action would involve trying to change the direction of our advanced economies, so that they can take on an increasing share of the processed agricultural produce and industrial products of the backward countries.

A move would be made to force our government leaders and industrialists to revalue their raw materials, by boycotting them if necessary (the Dutch have managed to stop people serving them coffee from Angola, that byword for oppression). They would also be forced to levy an international tax so that the flow of new capital to the deprived countries would be reversed and they would be given the basic equipment they need free of charge. The younger generation would teach immigrants working with them to read and write, as the students at the 'Agro' are doing now for their 'very own Third World'. They would also take part in any overseas campaign to promote literacy and offer training that could use their services, thus working out a totally new concept of teaching. They would live with the Africans and adopt their way of life, as the Chinese are already doing . . . .

This 'Third World' campaign would logically be tied up with nature conservation, ecology, the fight against pollution, the slaughter of animals, hunting, bullfighting etc. Instead of relying on some manufacturer of alcoholic drinks to finance them – he would merely be looking for some new and attractive way of advertising his product – the campaigners would try to stress the *political* nature of all these movements. If they are to be effective against all these forms of waste they must first insist on a fairer distribution of incomes, and must insist in the strongest possible terms on all the necessary measures for achieving greater social justice by gradual but continual stages.

We would then begin to realize that this type of movement is tied up with an attempt to find new ways of making the transition to a new concept of socialism – to a socialist system geared to survival. There's no longer any point, indeed it's no longer possible, if we look at it from the world view, in giving everyone *everything* he can ever want – or rather everything that current social structures have conditioned him to want. Instead we should aim to give him merely whatever he needs to live a full life – and that means a lot less. There's no question of money changing hands here. If services are rendered free this cuts out a lot of fiddly and unproductive work; for instance, free medicine does away with all those wretched bits of red tape for the Social Security.*

---

* In France those who are entitled to cheap medical treatment have to pay for all their medicine first and then fill up a claim form for a rebate (*translator's note*).

The first step, and the most difficult and urgent one, would be to seize the power that is at present in the hands of the privileged few in each country. This would be the specific task of today's younger generation, who would simply have to manage it somehow before our 'little planet' is damaged beyond repair, in other words before the end of this century. To strengthen them in their resolve they can look at the work done by the Club of Rome, which suggests that if the profit society continues it will inevitably lead to global catastrophe. Let me say yet again that it's high time we took *violent* action, since, in Robert Lattés's words, 'The ability of a system to weather a crisis dissolves when the phenomenon increases . . . as with the fight against pollution, famine and the irreparable damage that is being done to the environment.'[4]

We can thus envisage the possibility of singling out the privileged few who are responsible for the imminent final catastrophe, which will, adds Lattés, be triggered off by 'the spiral of population growth and economic development, which is constantly creating or increasing the gulf between nations or within society'. We could therefore show all our compatriots that those who are responsible for the profit economy must hand over the reins of power, since the path they're leading us along will inevitably end in the abyss. Then again we must be prepared to offer our young people an ambitious programme that will arouse their enthusiasm, and one that isn't more or less restricted to the internal problems of France, as was the joint programme put forward by the French Communist Party and the Socialist Party in 1972, or even that of the United Socialist Party (PSU).

If we look at the situation from the point of view of the whole planet, of mankind as a whole, our top priority will be to end waste in the rich countries, including such popular forms of waste as the family car; and also to end inequality, even when this is readily accepted, as with the affluence in which the rich live, thus insulting the poverty in the Third World. This would necessitate a long period of education so that the degree of awareness that is necessary if we are going to revise all our concepts can spread to large numbers of people. A schoolboy in Montargis remarked that this would mean the end of democracy. Today's society does admittedly allow a good deal of licence, but only in the rich countries, and even there it allows greater licence to the rich. Is that really what democracy is all about? On the international scale the rich represent an out-and-out oligarchy.

The political elimination of the privileged few will be brutal in some places and gradual elsewhere, as with Allende's experiment in Chile. Their ideology will always tend to rear its ugly head all over again, so the cultural revolution will have to be an ongoing process, which could be happily combined with a new type of permanent education. Admittedly the 'educational city' outlined in the Faure Report for UNESCO does represent an attempt at modernization, but it also spins out the concepts underlying the capitalist society. The Soviet writer Petrovski was right to stress the fact that 'it does not pay sufficient attention to the wealth of experiments in educational development in the USSR and the other socialist countries'. His comment would have been more valuable if instead of confining his remarks to Soviet-controlled central Asia he had also stressed the importance of the experiments going on in China, which the Report dismisses a few brief notes.

Yes, it seems to me that the Chinese experiment is indeed being carried out by the society that is most likely to survive for any length of time. The regiments of bicycles bowling down the broad avenues in Peking don't produce any smoke; the general interest is the main preoccupation of the very great majority of people; their rubbish is salvaged, there is a very high level of socialist conscience . . . . As I have shown on many occasions, this experiment is an extremely valuable one for the dominated countries, though they are not recommended to copy it slavishly, because they are starting out from a different set of conditions from every possible point of view. So what we must do now is to make the various different aspects of this experiment and the most important of its results known to a wider public, though not merely by official eulogies along somewhat tendentious lines, which ultimately lessen their impact – particularly because other nations often find them difficult to follow.

Our developed societies would undoubtedly find in China the basis of a new belief in man and his potential for progress. But the most important decisions, such as foreign policy or the Plan, are worked out at the very top of the hierarchy, within the inner circle of rulers. They are therefore invested with exceptional powers, without any sign at this level of the famous 'control by the people' that Lenin insisted on. As a result power-struggles in China are pretty tough and we know little of them except for the occasional vague rumble, as when Liu Chao-chi was toppled, or more recently when the same thing happened to Lin Piao and his supporters. Admittedly workers' control does play a much more important part than in the Soviet Union, but only on the local level, when it comes to implementing the major decisions on a regional basis. The workers are offered the chance to approve the major decisions as they are implemented, but they're told about them after they've been taken; they aren't consulted on major policy trends.

Some people have irreverently compared *The Little Red Book* to the catechism. Friends explained to me that if they were to shake off the dangerous and still very pronounced hold of the old society they couldn't let their supporters defend their various theses in public. All right, but there can be, there are and there always will be different concepts of socialism, different phases. If the Chinese knew more about what's going on in the outside world they would be in a better position to judge which version is best suited to their own country, and could claim the right to a share in working out the major decisions. Power is restricted in essence to a small number of people. China isn't the only example of this: after all, de Gaulle didn't ask what the French people thought before he vetoed Britain's application to enter the Common Market, and there are plenty of other examples. So let's salute the Chinese leaders for their devotion to the general interest and to that of the workers. If we prefer greater freedom of information and more democracy for ourselves, even if this is only a formal nod to democracy, it surely isn't up to us to say what's best for China, a country that our forefathers cynically exploited!

And don't let's forget what happened in Vietnam!

If they see that we're planning to isolate them the privileged few will defend themselves by counter-attacking, by getting in the first blow. The United States occupied Santo Domingo to prevent it turning into a second Cuba; Brazil helped the counter-revolution in Bolivia and Chile; the Soviet Union occupied Czechoslovakia because a form of socialism was being evolved there that rejected the idea of despotism and a small group of oligarchs enjoying unfair privileges. In each case the chances of their finishing up with democracy and the type of socialist system I've been trying to outline seem to be growing slimmer every day . . . .

The threat that the main resources, energy and metal-ores, plus fresh water and clean air, will soon run out should give them an incentive to distribute these resources on a more equal basis, if the idea of social justice got through to the majority of the population. But the same threat can also encourage the privileged countries (and in particular those with the most power) to find new ways of getting their hands on most of the earth's riches, by isolating the various forms of poverty to certain regions and thus closing their eyes to them. Because we granted a small share of them to the oligarchy in Brazil and gave a few crumbs to her police we are having to stand by and watch as the most odious system of repression in the modern era (it shares this honour with the system in South Vietnam, but that seems to be on its way out) is installed in Brazil.

This is where the part played by the manual workers, peasants, intellectuals and the whole of the working population in the rich countries could soon become decisive. If they refused *en masse* to accept this type of economic and political conditioning of the dominated countries, and the increasing plunder of the Third World, they could make an effective contribution to safeguarding their great-grandchildren's chances of survival, and of leading a life worth living. But Claude Poperen, who is a communist, is taking a step in the wrong direction when he sings the praises of the idea of everybody owning a private car. Which would make the privations and the plunder of the Third World even worse. Once people have started leading a cosy bourgeois life it's more difficult to recreate genuine international solidarity.

We should have to accept a degree of discipline and there-fore a new belief in the future. This new belief would possibly have to be secular, since Christianity, with its European-centrist overtones, has been pretty well disqualified in most of the dominated countries. The guide who showed me round the Duomo in Siena explained that the magnificent carvings on the pulpit could never have been sculpted so beautifully if the artist had been working for money. This isn't the Middle Ages any more. Yet a new belief in men, in the new man who has cast off the old avaricious and pretentious man who still slumbers inside most of us, could take us back there. He may have fewer personal possessions, but he will have a share in more communal possessions.

We might arrive at this state of having less but *being* more if we could set up communities that showed greater concern for all who live on this little planet. In that case anti-totalitarian solidarity would be strong enough to prevent us all sinking into chaos. But we haven't won yet, and we never will chalk up a permanent victory. Luckily for our great-grandchildren, whose life would have little attraction, little real interest in a society of universal and officially recognized beatitude, even if they had reached some version of the 'highest stage' of communism.

Yet the destiny of mankind has never been exposed to such great dangers, has never been confronted with the same difficulties as over the last 35 years, since 1938. Admittedly the danger of war between the two great powers seems to be waning, but if there were too great a *rapprochement* between them this could be a threat as well. The point is that these two super-powers now represent the two most dangerous forms of totalitarianism: that of a recurrent Stalinism which cannot be eradicated; and that of dominating imperialism by the rich countries, with their insatiable demands and their monstrous privileges. When it gets to the stage of covering up its exploits with a pseudo-democratic veil the hypocrisy of the United States reaches an all-time high, and fascism could easily take root behind the whole military and industrial complex.

'Hope changed sides and the mood of the battle changed.' We aren't with Victor Hugo at Waterloo any more, but the work done by the Club of Rome isn't the same as Grouchy serving the Bonapartist cause or Blücher fighting for British imperialism. If we play our cards right in the debate, and particularly if we expose the fact that 'our' civilization cannot survive long under capitalism, then we shall be able to show that we are being 'forced' into socialism.

8   *The conditions of global equilibrium geared to survival*

If the rich world is going to survive it cannot go on being rich, since its wealth is as unwarranted as it is inconsiderate. We are at this moment living out *the last decades of the wasteful society*. When I went to the FAO in Rome to collect some material and ideas for this book I got stuck in an even worse traffic jam in the centre of the old town at about 7 pm than in the centre of Paris, and I was immobilized longer – it was only too obvious that Baron Haussman had never got his hands on Rome and straightened out the streets as he did in Paris! When the level of pollution goes above the danger mark the people of Los Angeles are advised to avoid exerting themselves, so as not to breathe in too much polluted air. In Tokyo people sometimes wear gas-masks. We may well get to this stage throughout the planet. When that happens many of those who have failed to speak out will grasp the truth, but it will be too late, since there is no historical precedent for this threat. And we always tend to go solely on precedent.

People will say I'm being pessimistic, but I'm not. From the very first page of this book I too, like the Club of Rome, have been looking for a way out of the problem. But I haven't simply been trying to find one that would be viable over a longer period, as they have. I want one that would also be more humane and fairer than our declining and decadent capitalism, which the Club chose not to condemn. Their theoretical conclusions show that we can survive for a very long time in a state of global equilibrium, providing the following three conditions are fulfilled, and we must see that this happens in the near future:

1) *The capital plant and the population are constant in size.* The birth rate equals the death rate and the capital investment rate equals the depreciation rate.
2) *All input and output rates – births, deaths, investment and deprecia-*

*tion – are kept to a minimum.*

3) *The levels of capital and population and the ratio of the two are set in accordance with the values of society.*[5]

They point out that this kind of equilibrium does not mean stagnation, and that it allows either development or an end to certain types of activity, as the case may be; a redistribution of population; 'income could be more or less evenly distributed . . . . No one can predict what sort of institutions man might develop under these new conditions.'[6]

Admittedly to act differently would be to indulge in prophecy. But these conclusions in no way prohibit us from pursuing man's age-old dream of a fairer society, bits of which are coming true at various points on the globe, in spite of setbacks elsewhere. Our children would accept the necessary sacrifices more readily if they could glimpse some possibility of building a society that could offer a certain 'quality of life'. I should call this a 'society without contempt'.

9   *A society without contempt, or imperfect socialism, with no prospect of communism*

If contempt were thought of as a mortal sin, as the one absolutely unacceptable failing, everyone would recover the dignity of the man who is respected whatever his race, his colour, his age, his sex, his income, his rank, his status, his class, his religion, his opinions or his education – the only exceptions being contempt for and exploitation of others (the one leads to the other). Many a Fourierist dream has failed, and I'm not going to recommend yet another one. The history of capitalism is itself full of failure, yet one day it 'flowered' into industrial development. This flowering was restricted to the privileged few, and it is leading us all to catastrophe . . . .

Socialism begins with a series of relative failures; we have examined a few examples of such failures. Yet all these 'attempts' give us an opportunity to look for some guidance and we must make the best possible use of all these experiments, some of which have been expensive for the ordinary people involved, as in the Soviet Union or even in Cuba.

149

There's China, which has produced new men as strong as steel, and so many of them that we're entitled to feel more hopeful. The young people who reject our consumer society are in some cases organizing themselves into fringe groups on the edges of the consumer society, though admittedly they're sponging on it to a certain extent. But it's a start, and it will be followed by other experiments that will go a little further each time until they're in a position to influence the whole of society. Yugoslavia is following her independent line in the face of considerable difficulties, and some aspects of her policy represent a return to capitalism, but that's no reason for condemning her outright. And Vietnam has forced the most powerful nation in the world to withdraw.

What I want to do in this section is to rough out a few quick 'sketches' in coloured chalks to encourage my readers to think about various possibilities. They will have to be effectively put into practice, though such experiments must inevitably involve a good deal of feeling one's way, before we can advance any further. Our capitalist society has admittedly resulted in fantastic material progress, thanks to the way science has mastered nature – which meant it could also plunder her! – and because it has reduced the poor to a condition that Helder Camara rightly refers to as subhuman. And without the slightest concern either for those who will come after us, and for whom we are responsible, or even for the most wretched people of our own time, for whom we are even more directly responsible.

Capitalist society has proved to be incapable of perfecting a society that respects the dignity of all men, not only by helping the rich to flourish, as they are today, but by doing the same for all of us. This could be achieved only if everyone put all his abilities at the service of community groups organized on a local, regional, national and worldwide basis. The logical follow-up to the new type of school with part-time manual labour – with work that is instructive and interesting, rather than soul-destroying – would be a new system for allocating work, under which everyone would do his share of 'servile' jobs, such as cleaning or refuse collection. This could start in the rural communes or in areas of a town where people already have a well-developed community spirit.

Some will say that under this system a doctor would be wasting his valuable time, since his primary function is to care for the sick, which is what they said about the first worker-priests. This is perfectly true as long as there are so few doctors and they're so precious. But in France they're trying to cut down the number of doctors by failing a large number of students at the Faculté de Médicine in Paris in 1972 who would have deserved to pass. The Doctors' Union wants to keep the numbers of practising doctors down so as to guarantee their privileges and their fees, which are sometimes exorbitantly high – though they finish up being overworked.

When there's a surplus of people trained to work with their brains we'll finally get what we want, for everyone will be able to benefit from a continuous process of education, which will eventually take the place of today's universities. When this happens it would be logical for everyone to do his share of manual work. Views on class, hierarchy and contempt for the poor will change when all these 'mandarins' are working side by side, hand in hand, and eating in the same canteen (the word 'companion' comes from Latin *cum panem,* 'with bread') with people who previously they only too often thought of as 'them'. Groups of workmates would find it easier to achieve what the army, that oppressive society, has never managed to achieve, particularly if they went to the same 'work-school'.

This society without contempt would channel the organized pressure of public opinion (China is showing us how influential this can be when it is inspired by a new 'faith') into the fight against all forms of waste and pollution. Large families would soon be discredited, even before penalties were brought in; eventually they would be illegal. But it would be Utopian (there, I've fallen into the trap!) to think that a society of this kind could become truly angelic and do without rules and discipline, power and institutions.

The kind of democracy I'm trying to rough out here has never really been put into practice. It could still win its spurs, but only if it is properly realized in depth, the first step being to allow complete freedom of expression and full information for everybody, rather along the lines of the 'libertarian, anarcho-trade-unionist and self-governing socialism' put forward by Edmond Maire on 17 October 1972.* In many countries a minimum of education would have to be provided for everyone before this could be implemented.

* Edmond Maire became General-Secretary of one of France's three trade union federations, the Conféderation française du travail (CFDT), in 1971 (*translator's note*).

Contradictions appear at every turn, between on the one hand the need, not for a world government, which would involve too much centralization, but for supranational bodies to take charge of the economy in each of the groups that go to make up the world, and on the other hand the need to decentralize the maximum number of decisions even further, so that everyone can have a share in decision-taking. The neo-Fourierist schemes that might be adopted won't be able, any more than nations are, to take sole charge of their territory, because they'll have to respect the worldwide requirements for survival. These should definitely not lead to niggling and bureaucratic regulations, and there ought to be a much freer dialogue between the government and the governed than at present. Measures will have to be taken to make sure that everyone respects the general interest, but also to make sure that the authorities are controlled by those over whom they exercise authority. Lenin attached great importance to this form of control from below, since those with the power are always liable to abuse it.

It's extremely difficult to envisage this society, in which no one will be despised and yet which will not be perfect. Abundance, will never be achieved; the nearest to it will be a series of evolutions. It will always be a place of conflict, in which man's aggressive impulses should be guided into new channels rather than curbed; he should be able to give them free rein, as in sexual or sporting contests, especially in the latter case when things get out of hand!

But most important, don't let's envisage our future in the gloomy light that might be conjured up by the very word 'austerity', because this curb on consumption will enable those who are worst-off today to lead a comfortable life. The quality of life will depend on the conditions in which we live and on our personal relationships rather than on the possessions we accumulate, as soon, that is, as all of us can eat decently, dress decently and live in decent surroundings – and this will be perfectly possible if we keep our numbers down. We shall all be able to live in a 'teaching city' in which everyone will both learn and teach, simultaneously and constantly. Respect for nature will give us an opportunity to get to know her better and to appreciate her, to live in harmony with all other living organisms – plants and animals, forests and woods and streams, the winds and the waves.

Painters, even Sunday painters, will be able to concentrate

152

on their favourite occupation, decorating their surroundings, and other artists will be able to organize non-stop shows, in which the streets and the whole village will be *en fête*. These are only suggestions, since future generations will decide what is to happen. But we should leave them a wider area of choice by clearing away the main obstacles and mental blocks and getting rid of the most harmful types of privilege. You may think that what I've said here doesn't go far enough, but I was reluctant to go any further.

The first tentative attempts by the socialist systems that are in operation today are inevitably less satisfactory than the ones I've outlined here. All they can do is give us a few hints about how to work out various models of socialism geared to the survival of the planet, though they will also have to fulfil a large number of other conditions. Each social group will be invited to set up its own structures more or less as it thinks fit, but also bearing in mind the situation it has inherited (development, mentality, sociology, education etc.), and in particular the new constraints resulting from the shortage of resources throughout the world.

Each unit would be able, by means of dialogues, discussions and conflicts, sweat and tears (maybe blood, too), and bearing in mind the factors outlined above, to work out which social model is most appropriate for its members, after consulting them on a democratic basis. But this model will have to take the constraints into account. It is essential that the various plans should be constantly shuttled back and forth between the grass-roots and the national and supranational organizations; and some form of arbitration machinery will have to be perfected . . . . If the State as a constraining force were devalued there would certainly have to be some sort of institution for arbitrating disputes.

Each society will thus be able to work out its own version of an imperfect socialist system that can be re-examined and corrected at frequent intervals, selecting one that will fit in with its various aspirations and yet will enable it to survive. There would therefore be a whole series of competing socialist models, and there would be no need for anyone to go round saying that his particular version was the only one with the right outlook. But these various models, these different methods of transition could not include the prospect of a communist society in which everything was in plentiful supply, since that now seems out of the question. The concept of 'to each according to his needs' can no longer be applied, except in the case of *reasonable* needs – food, clothing, housing, ongoing education, leisure and travel. In other words, such needs must be limited, so that everyone can have his fair share, black men and yellow men included.

Trying to make people understand that we must first take care of the worst-off and of future generations is a thankless task. It will be difficult to persuade those who are bent on reform and those who are or claim to be revolutionaries to join forces and fight a genuine battle on behalf of the Third World. And what sort of a battle will it be?

## 10   *One last attempt at a conclusion*

Now that I've got to the end of this short essay I can see even more clearly how inadequate it is, even though I did say this right at the start. Ultimately the problem is above all a political one. But it is turning out to be too difficult to be left to the politicians, not to mention those who are in power now. A large number of men and women from differing walks of life and different social backgrounds, but united in their concern for the future of mankind and eager to promote the fairest possible sort of society, would have to embark on this 'great work' as well. They would be guided by the dual prospect of survival and social justice, which are now the prime targets.

The first stage would be designed to convince the majority of people in each country, starting with the rich nations. This would raise the dual problem of education, which would have to be rethought entirely, and information, which would have to be freed from the political propaganda spewed out by the authorities, or from the economic overlordship of the rich and the advertisers – this applies equally to Paris, London, Moscow or Washington. The heightened awareness that would result from this would enable us to lay siege more effectively to the existing powers, and to make them more clearly aware of their responsibilities and of their short-sightedness.

If they won't accept the necessary structural changes, if they won't listen to the arguments of the boldest reformers they'll be toppled by revolutions. In the words of Claude Gruson, 'If one day revolutions become politically inevitable this will probably be because the reformers weren't imaginative enough. Or because they couldn't get the authorities to understand what they were getting at.'[7]

It seems to me that in the short term this lack of understanding is the most likely of the two reasons, and the dominated countries are becoming increasingly aware of this. It seems more likely every day that revolutions will occur. It would be a good thing if we could prevent them from causing an unbearable level of pollution, nuclear cataclysm and uncontrollable climatic upsets. Let's hope that the first catastrophes will be on a relatively minor scale, yet impressive enough to convince people of the need to accept discipline and to make the privileged few give up their privileges – which they will when they realize that these privileges are leading them to suicide along with everyone else.

Let's hope that this new awareness won't come too late, because the race to the death is already on and our chances of survival are dwindling every day. The terror that was felt as the Year One Thousand approached has a strange resonance at the end of this second millennium, but this time there's nothing irrational about it. Yet the ability of the human race to adapt, its powers of imagination and invention will be able to pull us out of many a tight corner – as long as things haven't gone too far.

Will the 'new man' who will be thrown up by militant action and the new system of ongoing education discover a new secular religion capable of producing leaders who are more utterly devoted to the interests of humanity, and will thus give first priority to the interests of the worst-off sectors of the community? Will this new religion be able to inspire the sort of devotion found in certain monks in the Middle Ages, or in certain cadres within the various communist parties, the Canbô in Vietnam or in China? Will these executives be capable, in spite of the inevitable mistakes (which are clearly revealed in William Hinton's book *Fanshen*[8] as far as the process of land reform in China goes), of making the masses accept the necessary disciplines?

Incidentally, these disciplines could be very largely outweighed by a way of life, a setting, a quality of life vastly superior to our unthinking selfishness. We can still build a pleasant, relaxed and tranquil society in tune with nature. But only the future can offer us a series of solutions, each of which will be inadequate. The future hasn't yet been written – it will depend on my younger readers, to whom I say: you will be rewarded individually for the results of your collective action; the militants will fight on behalf of the others, but if you don't give them enough support they'll be defeated. But don't for goodness' sake start out with a defeatist attitude.

We must shake off our belief in a scientific truth that is leading us to a predetermined future. If you substitute ideas for reality you no longer need to justify your actions – and that can lead yet again to some form of neo-Stalinism. The objective of a society in which people are mentally interdependent and there are fewer inequalities must prevail over that of making more and more goods available. How can we learn about the dangers threatening us all at the least possible cost? Must we consign the privileged few to oblivion, or can we arrange things so that they feel the need to join sides with the rest of us? (This paragraph was suggested to me by G. Séverac.)

On the other hand, Raymonde Étienne reminds me that world planning could be organized to the advantage of an international privileged minority, if ordinary working people hadn't seized power first and put an end to capitalism and imperialism. I'm afraid things will never be as simple as that. We'll have to nibble slowly away at all these selfish attitudes one by one, within firms, within nations and ultimately on the international level. The battle that will have to be fought will require a good deal more intelligence and will have to confront dogmatic and over-simplified attitudes.

Yet everyone would have to become aware of his responsibilities more quickly. All those who cling on to the privileges of the consumer society, who refuse to accept the structural reforms that must be carried through if we are to survive and if social justice is to be achieved throughout the world, can from now on be thought of as murderers – their victims being the worst-off sectors of the community. Do you want to run the risk of being treated as a murderer by your own children, who are going to be more aware of what is going on because methods of education will have changed?

Let me end with three quotations:

The first is from Louis Aragon's obituary on the journal

*Lettres françaises,* which was killed by the communists because it was too intractable. Speaking on 11 October, 1972, he said: '[My] life is like some terrible game in which I was on the losing side; I've ruined it from beginning to end.' I wouldn't want my younger readers to be reduced to writing something along those lines when they're 75, as Aragon is today.

Secondly, the casualty figures for the Vietnam War printed by the *Washington Globe* on 27 October, 1972 – when it was thought to be over:

> 46,000 Americans (plus 303,000 missing)
> 900,000 Vietnamese soldiers
> 4,300,000 Vietnamese civilians

The preponderance of civilian dead is revealing.

Thirdly, a passage from an article in *Ceres* by Probhat Roy:

> Forced to live in these deplorable conditions of utter misery and destitution, the poor and the weak *have hardly any will or initiative left.* And even if they are agile and active, they are constantly pushed down to rock bottom physical existence by the scourges of hunger, disease, illiteracy and the octopus of indebtedness. Moreover, traditional practices, sway of caste or community inhibitions or restrictions and age-old prejudices dull them to such an extent that new ideas can hardly penetrate their armour of resistance. Thus, in the end, they reduce themselves to be *mere beasts of burden* rather than socially productive *human beings. Such are harsh realities surrounding the life of the poor farmers of India.*
>
> Collectively, the village life is still – even after decades of capitalist penetration – characterized by a diluted form of semi-feudalistic structure. Few rich families – because of their prized land, caste superiority, education and relative afflence – effectively control all the levers of power, both social and economic. They are the moneylenders, usurers, traders, bankers and government agents. They hold important positions in local institutions financed or controlled by governments . . . . [9]

All of *us* are responsible for this abject poverty. We shall have to smash the system, starting with our own countries.

Yes, I know, I belong to the privileged minority. So this book is also a piece of self-criticism. I'm doing my best, but we'll have to change an awful lot of institutions and structures if we want to get going faster.

In his review *Croissance des jeunes nations,* which often makes some good points, G. Blardonne recalls the argument put forward in a 1977 FAO report by M. Cépède: the nations with a rapidly growing population are stepping up their level of agricultural output faster. This line of reasoning has not been verified by the facts, and neither Mr Cépède nor the FAO has used it again. Blardonne, who was writing at the end of 1972, would have been more up to date if he'd quoted A. Boerma's most recent statement that we can already predict that the second decade of development will be one of failure in agriculture (see part I, section 6). I've just come back from Bangladesh, where the food shortages are getting worse all the time as the population figures rise (this was true even before the recent tragedies). Her neighbour India, who was able to fight a war in 1971, the only year when she didn't have to import any grain (thanks to the fact that half her population was more or less starving), is having to start buying grain all over again.

Everyone's always going on about the brilliant results of the experiments with cooperatives in Comilla, to the east of Bangladesh, where hundreds of experts and thousands of local trained personnel have been struggling with remarkable persistence against underdevelopment, and particularly against money-lending, since 1961. In all the villages I visited round Comilla in January 1973 private money-lending was still practised. In Mathurapur, which has an agricultural population of 900 to the square kilometre, the average farm covers less than one acre and the village produces 100–120 kilos of rice per capita per annum. The large mango-trees are cut down at the height of the productive season so that the villagers can survive, yet the timber from them will scarcely bring them in more than the annual income they can get from the fruit. Those who don't own any land want to get out, but where can they go? Meanwhile for 3 months in the year they eat only one meal a day. The family I interviewed – they had four tiny children – had borrowed 180 kilograms of rice in December 1972. To pay for it they'll have to hand over 600 kilograms of rice to the ubiquitous money-lender. It's already perfectly obvious that they'll never be able to do it, so they'll be in debt for the rest of their lives.

In the village of Chowogram, 250 kilometres north-east of Dacca, 200 out of the 2,500 villagers – a record – have passed or almost passed the school-leaving exam, but haven't been able to find any office work. They're living off their parents and their brothers, doing literally nothing all the year round – and yet there's so much to be done. The World Bank anticipates that there will be '140–170 million Bengalis in the year 2000 [there are 75 or 80 million now and the official growth rate is 3 per cent per annum; according to my most recent estimates it will be 39 per cent in 11 years] with an overall rate of employment in rural areas of 30 per cent, which is liable to remain at that level for the next 30 years'!

Since every 1,000 people in California take away 1 square kilometre of farming land, if the 'American way of life' were implemented here there wouldn't be any land left to cultivate. The World Bank has published the most vehement criticisms of the Club of Rome's work, but Aurelio Peccei and Manfred Siebker gave them as good as they got in a paper presented to the Council of Europe. It's easy to see why a report stressing that representatives of the rich nations are demolishing the whole planet didn't get a favourable reception from the representatives of those nations.

The growing carbon-dioxide content in the atmosphere represents the most serious threat of all. The best way of checking it is to see that the excess is absorbed by some form of vegetation that won't decompose, by some well-preserved wood, which can be used as timber and for ship-building – like all those thousands of sailing and rowing junks that are such a delightful sight at the mouth of the Ganges and the river Jamuna (part of the Brahmaputra). But then we mustn't go on clearing forests; we could try to grow orchards and food-bearing trees, but we mustn't turn them all into arable land – so that will once again limit our agricultural potential. Like the other species of living creatures man must learn to set limits for himself – or else we can expect the most terrible catastrophes. Where can we find pilots who don't suffer from short sight?

And now go off and read an article called 'Le capitalisme périphérique' ('Peripheral Capitalism') printed in *Tiers Monde* at the end of 1972. And go and see *Winter Soldier*, a film in which American soldiers who fought in Vietnam express their anguish by accusing themselves of having committed the worst possible atrocities there. What are the chances of

the rich countries repeating this attempt to reduce the poor
countries to a state of bondage?

# POSTSCRIPT TO THE
# ENGLISH EDITION
# (EARLY 1974)

This essay was first published in 1973 and was written at great speed between July and November 1972 under the violent impact of the initial conclusions reached by the Club of Rome. Its impact was of course less violent for those who were constantly warning people about the growing danger of widespread famine in the Third World – which in my case means since 1966.[1] But the impact was still great, for it sketched out in greater detail the possibility, or even the probability, that the majority of the dominated countries would continue to be poor in perpetuity. The dramatic famine has already got too great a hold, from the western Sahara in West Africa to Ethiopia, after the Indian famine of 1965–6. Chronic famine is also affecting increasing numbers of unfortunate people, particularly in India and Bangladesh, in Java, in the Peruvian Andes and the Nordeste region in Brazil – which has not yet been rescued by the Brazilian 'miracle'.

The privileged minorities who take unfair advantage of their position – and particularly the largest of them, those in the so-called developed countries, those belonging to 'central capitalism', who plunder the Third World and squander their material wealth, which does not fetch a high enough price in spite of its relative scarcity – refused, and indeed still refuse, to understand that the night of 4 August is rapidly approaching for the privileged few.* But now they've been put on their guard by the energy crisis, by the problems of the price of oil,

* See translator's note on p. 68.

and still more recently by the collapse of our monetary system – two facts that I heralded in this essay. Incidentally, I have deliberately left it largely as it first appeared, which means that the reader should always bear in mind the date when it was written.

The energy crisis is at last enabling the dominated countries to appreciate the full validity and strength of the proverb 'united we stand, divided we fall'. This applies equally to other raw materials such as phosphates (which I've already referred to), and will soon apply to bauxite, iron ore, tin, rare metals, copper and so on. The Inter-governmental Council of Copper-exporting Countries has already brought together the four large copper exporters (Zaire, Zambia, Chile and Peru), and it was essential to nip in the bud an organization that was liable to gain economic strength, and therefore political strength, from the defection of Chile. Sordid interests were therefore hidden behind a mask of pseudo-'Christian' morality. And why shouldn't an 'OPEC' for fats, coffee, tea and cocoa, natural rubber and so on be set up in the near future?

The crisis is having a serious effect on the poor countries that have no oil of their own, and the motor-pumps that are needed to irrigate the intensive winter rice, the *irri boro* of Bangladesh, have already ground to a halt because the country hasn't got enough foreign currency to pay for the necessary fuel-oil. And also because they haven't taken into account my recommendations for urban austerity. The crisis is going to test the Third World's solidarity: are the *nouveaux riches* countries, whose wealth is based on oil, going to behave as badly – or even worse – towards the 'damned of this earth' as we 'old rich' countries have? We must keep a careful eye on the situation.

In our countries with their age-old wealth, with their long-standing middle class, there is no longer any question of extending the privileges of the said middle class to the whole population. In asking for a growth rate higher than the rate predicted by the government, the Common Programme of the French Left, drawn up in 1972–3, would have insisted on an even greater increase in the amount of oil imported from the Arab countries. Now the official programmes of the developed countries, ranging from Japan to Western Europe, were demanding an increase of 15 per cent per annum. Which was already sheer lunacy and quite unattainable on our little planet, so limited in its reserves and already overpopulated.

If our economic system continues to be controlled by market forces, now that the days of cheap oil are over the poor will have to do without heating – and large numbers of manual workers will be out of work, while Mercedes, Citroëns and Chevrolets will still be on the roads, cocking a snook at their poverty. In France the ratio of the incomes of the wealthiest 10 per cent of the population to the poorest 10 per cent is the highest in Europe – 76:1 according to P. Drouin, writing in *Le Monde*. This means that we must cut down on our privileges instead of trying to offer them to larger numbers of people. We must ration oil; maintain the price of petrol at the present level for those who need it for manufacturing and distribution, but make everyone else pay much more for it; cut back on non-essential lighting and heating in shops and offices, regardless of their size; step up the output of firewood (by planting trees); and use the wind and geothermic energy, and particularly solar energy, rather than concentrating on nuclear energy alone, and so on; we must also widen our canals and increase our railway network, and use them to their full capacity; mass-produce barges and railway carriages, cars and coaches instead of private cars; ban cars with a high cylinder capacity in the very near future, together with motor-racing, since high speeds are no longer desirable and never will be again; we must put a stop to work on Concorde and halt nuclear tests, no matter where they are held.

The workforce that would be relased in this way could enable us to give the Third World the digging tools, irrigation equipment and machine-tools they so urgently need; to cut the terrible accelerating rhythm of assembly-line working and the length of the working week in our own countries; to distribute the right to work and to enjoy leisure – which must become the modern term for unemployment – evenly over the whole population. We would then have to see whether capitalism is capable of adapting itself in this way, of undergoing such a drastic series of structural reforms. If it turns out not to be, we must replace it with a different system, and quickly, since there is a serious risk that the damage that is currently being done to the environment and to the planetary climate will reach the point of no return within about ten years. I may not be able to produce any evidence to substantiate this figure, but nor can the people who are busy demolishing our planet produce any evidence to show that I'm wrong. Now it's surely up to them to prove their case, since they're the ones who are going to be given a stiff sentence by the court of history.

P.S. In February 1974 Norman Borlaugh and Lester Brown, who instigated and championed the 'Green Revolution', told us that there is a great danger that the famine will spread in the next few years, since the grain stocks have run out. But the United States have leaned heavily on the Indian government to persuade them to delay the social changes that are essential if the rural masses are to be mobilized to produce a 'Chinese-style' workforce. India's average per capita output of basic foodstuffs for the years 1970–3 was 210 kilograms, compared to 330 kilograms in China. India has 27 per cent of her land under irrigation, compared to 77 per cent in China. The political consequences of the difference between the two figures will not always be covered up by foreign 'aid'.

# NOTES AND REFERENCES

*End of a Civilization*
1 Barbara Ward and René Dubos, *Only One Earth. The care and maintenance of a small planet* (London: Deutsch 1972); Robert Lattés, *Pour une autre croissance* (Paris: Le Seuil 1972); Barry Commoner, *Closing Circle: The Environmental Crisis and Its Cure* (London: Cape 1972); Dennis Meadows et al., *Limits to Growth: A report for the Club of Rome's project on the Predicament of Mankind* (London: Earth Island 1972); The *Ecologist, A Blueprint for Survival* (Harmondsworth: Penguin 1972).
2 Patrick François, *Bulletin de Nutrition* (of Food and Agriculture Organization of the United Nations), 9: 4 (1971) (French edn only).
3 André Clément Decouflé, *La Prospective,* in *Que sais-je?* series (Paris: Presses Universitaires de France 1972).


*Part I*
1 Colin Clark, *Starvation or Plenty* (London: Secker & Warburg 1970), pp. 168 and 171.
2 Herman Kahn and Anthony J. Wiener, *The Year Two Thousand. A framework for speculation on the next thirty-three years* (New York: Macmillan; London: Collier-Macmillan 1969).
3 Meadows et al., *Limits to Growth,* p. 19.
4 *Ibid.,* pp. 22, 23.
5 Barbara Ward, in conversation with the author.

6 Commoner, *Closing Circle.*
7 Dumont, *Lands Alive,* transl. Suzanne and Gilbert Sale (London: Merlin 1965).
8 Samir Amin, 'L'Afrique sous-peuplée', *Développement et Civilisations* (March/June 1972).
9 FAO, *Provisional Indicative World Plan for Agricultural Development* (Rome 1969).
10 A. Boerma, as quoted in the *New York Times* of 21 November, 1972.
11 Jacques Cousteau, in *Paris-Match* (19 August 1972); cf. 'Vue économique des problèmes marins', a study by Bertrand de Jouvenel for Pacem in Maribus, a congress of marine biologists which stressed the dangers of pollution. Cf. also Clarence P. Idyll, *Farming the Sea: fact and fancy, Ceres,* V: 4 (1972).
12 Commoner, *Closing Circle.*
13 Cousteau, in *Paris-Match* (19 August 1972).
14 Dorst, *La Nature, problème politique* (Paris: Desclée de Brouwer 1971).
15 A. Sasson, unpublished paper, Science Faculty, University of Rabat.
16 Robin Clarke, *The Science of War and Peace* (London: Jonathan Cape 1971).
17 *Ibid.,* 137-9.
18 Commoner, *Science and Survival* (London: Gollancz; New York: Viking 1966), pp. 68, 69.


Part II
1 Alfred Sauvy, *Les quatres roues de la fortune* (Paris: Flammarion 1968).
2 *Japan Times,* quoted in *Le Monde* (27-8 August, 1972).
3 P. R. and A. H. Ehrlich, *Population, Resources and Environment: issues in human ecology* (San Francisco: W. H. Freeman 1970), pp. 84-5.
4 Claude Julien, *Le Suicide des démocraties* (Paris: Grasset 1972).


Part III
1 Arghiri Emmanuel, *Unequal Exchange: a study of the imperialism of trade,* transl. Brian Pearce (London: NLB 1972); Gunder Frank, *Le développement du sous-développement*
166

(Paris: Maspéro 1970); Samir Amin, *L'accumulation à l'échelle mondiale* (Anthropos 1960); Pierre Jalée, *The Pillage of the Third World*, transl. Mary Klopper (New York and London: Monthly Review Press 1968); Paul Bairoch, *Le Tiers-Monde dans l'Impasse* (Paris: Gallimard 1971); Tibor Mende, *De l'aide à la recolonisation: les leçons d'un échec* (Paris: Le Seuil 1972).

2 'UN "shock report" on poverty', *Ceres,* 5: 4 (July/August 1972), p. 13; my italics.
3 Published in 1972 by the Futuribles Group, 52 rue des Saint-Pères, Paris 6e.
4 Unpublished thesis (now in press).
5 Philippe Gavi, *Le Triangle Indien* (Paris: Le Seuil 1972).
6 Jacques Gernet, *Le Monde Chinois* (Paris: A. Colin 1972).
7 *New Statesman* (19 December, 1959).
8 See Dumont, *Is Cuba Socialist?* (London: Deutsch 1974) and *Sovkhoz, Kolkhoz ou le problématique communisme* (Paris: Le Seuil 1964).
9 *Paysanneries aux abois* (Paris: Le Seuil 1972).

## Part IV

1 Quoted by Serge Mallet in *Critique Socialiste* (September/October 1972).
2 *Le Monde* (3–4 September 1972).
3 The *Ecologist, Blueprint for Survival,* pp. 37–8.
4 *Ibid.,* p. 39.
5 *Ibid.,* pp. 37–8.
6 *Ibid.,* p. 38.
7 J. L. Lavallard, 'Des stations d'épuration pour aider la nature', *Le Monde* (16 August 1972).
8 Aurelio Peccei, 'L'automobile contre les hommes', *Preuves,* II (1971).
9 Dumont, *Paysanneries aux abois.*
10 Michel Gutelman, *Réforme ou mystification agraire, le cas du Mexique* (Paris: Maspéro 1971).
11 Dumont, *Paysanneries aux abois.*

## Part V

1 Tibor Mende, 'Le Tiers Monde, victime de la croissance?', *Le Monde* (21 September 1972).
2 Marc Penouil, 'La Communauté économique ouest-

africaine, réalité actuelle ou espoir à long terme?', *Le Monde diplomatique* (September 1972).

3 Roy Medvedev, *Let History Judge: the origins and consequences of Stalinism,* transl. Colleen Taylor, ed. D. Joravsly and Georges Haupt (London: Macmillan 1972; New York: Knopf 1971).

4 Robert Lattés, *Pour une autre croissance* (Paris: Le Seuil 1973).

5 Dennis Meadows *et al., Limits to Growth,* pp. 173-4.

6 *Ibid.,* p. 174.

7 Claude Gruson, *L'Express* (11 September 1972).

8 William Hinton, *Fanshen: a documentary of revolution in a Chinese village* (Harmondsworth: Penguin 1972).

9 *Ceres,* 5: 5 (September/October 1972), p. 41; my italics.


*Postscript to the English edition*
1 Dumont and Bernard Rosier, *The Hungry Future,* transl. Rosamund Linell and R. B. Sutcliffe (London: Deutsch 1969).

# SELECT BIBLIOGRAPHY

Claude Bourdet, *A qui appartient Paris?* (Paris: Le Seuil 1972)
*L'Europe en l'an 2000* (Paris: Fayard 1972)
P. Georges, *L'environnement,* in *Que sais-je?* series (Paris: Presses Universitaires de France).
Jacques Gernet, *Le Monde chinois* (Paris: A. Colin 1972)
Jean Hamburger, *La Puissance et la fragilité* (Paris: Flammarion 1972)
François Hetman, *La Maitrise du futur* (Paris: Le Seuil 1971)
Jean Lacouture, *The Demigods: charismatic leadership in the third world,* transl. Patricia Wolf (London: Secker & Warburg 1971)
Bertrand de Jouvenel, *Arcadie: essais sur le mieux vivre* (Paris: SEDEIS 1968)
Konrad Lorenz, *Essais sur le comportement animal et humain* (Paris: Le Seuil 1970)
Paul Meiler, *Le Pensée utopique de William Morris* (Paris: Editions Sociales 1972)
Lewis Mumford, *The City in History* (London: Secker & Warburg 1961; Harmondsworth: Penguin 1966)
Karl Gunnar Myrdal, *The Challenge of World Poverty: a world anti-poverty program in outline* (New York: Pantheon; London: Allen Lane 1970)
Nguyen Khac Vien, *Expérience vietnamienne* (Paris: Editions sociales 1970)
F. Oury and J. Pain, *Chronique de l'école-caserne* (Paris: Maspéro 1972)
Georges Picht, *Réflexions au bord du gouffre* (Paris: Laffont 1970)

Michel Rocard, *Questions à l'état socialiste* (Paris: Stock 1972)
P. de Saint-Marc, *Socialisation de la nature* (Paris: Stock 1971)
Alvin Töffler, *Future Shock* (London: Bodley Head 1970)

*Ceres,* the FAO's monthly Review on Development, prints
    some outspoken articles
*Tiers Monde,* a journal published by the Presses Universitaires
    de France (Paris), see article *Le Capitalisme périphérique*
*Analyse et Prévisions,* a journal run by the Futuribles group,
    52 rue des Saint-Pères, Paris 6e

# INDEX

Africa: agriculture in, 19, 25, 121–2; emigrants from, 41–2, 43, 137; false start of, 81; food shortage in, 27, 77, 118, 161; illiteracy in, 58; Indians in, 41; proposals for, 85, 142; rebels in, 81; unemployment in, 138; *and see* South Africa, individual African countries

Agnelli Foundation, 53

Alexander, M., 28

Algeria: agriculture in, 20, 23; blocking of dams in, 24; French relations with, 1, 88; military expenditure of, 36; oil production in, 92

Allende, President, 35–6, 144

Amin, General, 41, 43

Amin, Samir, 18–19, 72

Anaconda, 91

Anglo-Iranian Oil Co., 91n

Angola, 81, 141

Annecy, Lake, 32

Antarctic Ocean, 30–1

Aragon, Louis, 156–7

Argentina, 88n, 121

Aron, Raymond, 14

Asia: employment in, 74; food shortages in, 27, 118; illiteracy in, 58; population of, 41, 42–3, 62, 132; *and see* individual Asian countries

Asians, Ugandan, 43

Assam, 75

Aswan Dam, 24

Atlantic Ocean: pollution of, 31; salmon in, 30, 124; trade winds of, 126

Australia, 42, 55, 122

Azienda Italiana Petroli (AGIP), 91

Bairoch, Paul, 72, 74

Baltic Sea, pollution of, 31

Bangladesh: cooperatives in, 158; famine in, 75, 118, 128, 158, 161; over-population of, 41, 43; poverty of, 162

Basle, 14

Belgium, 115

Bengal: famine in, 17; Naxalites in, 81; over-population of, 62, 100, 159; water wastage in, 24

Blardonne, G., 158

Boerma, A., 23, 99, 158

Borlaugh, Norman, 18, 164

tionaries of, 14–15; urbanization of, 61, 62; and whaling, 31

Java, over-population of, 41, 42, 62

Johnson, President Lyndon B., 3, 55

Julien, Claude: *Le Suicide des démocraties*, 63

Kahn, Herman, and Wiener, Anthony J., *Year Two Thousand*, 3, 9

Kenya, 25

Khrushchev, Nikita, 16

Korea, 38, 125

Latin America: counter-revolutions in, 146; food shortage in, 27, 50, 118, 161; illiteracy in, 60; immigration to, 41; population of, 38, 42, 132; rebel movements in, 81; regimes of, 18, 47, 92, 120–1; *and see* individual Latin American countries

Lattés, Robert: *Pour une autre Croissance*, 2, 51, 143

League of Nations, 118

Lecoin, Louis, 102

Lenin, V. I., 12, 84, 128, 141, 145, 152

*Lettres Françaises*, 156–7

Libya, 92

Lima Declaration (1971), 69

Lin Piao, 34, 145

Liu Chao-chi, 145

London, air pollution in, 31, 62

Los Angeles, air pollution in, 32, 54, 148

Loterie Nationale, 58

Lukacs, Georg, 66

McNamara, Robert S., 44, 71

Mahler, M., 18

Maire, Edmond, 151

Malaysia, 75

Mali, 24n, 57, 88, 132

Mao Tse-tung, 141; *Little Red Book*, 145

Marx, Karl, 67–8, 97, 141

Mattei, Enrico, 91 & n

Mauritania, 91, 123, 132

Mauritius, 41, 88n

Mazoyer, M., 2

Mediterranean Sea, 30; coast of, 22, 24

Medvedev, Roy: *Let History Judge*, 135

Melbourne, 122

Mende, Tibor, 72, 97, 129–30, 133

Mexico, 15, 18

Middle East: birth control in, 38; malnutrition in, 118; oil production in, 92, 162; war in, 82, 102

Miferma, 91

*Monde, Le*, 17, 72, 128, 163

Monjauze, Alexis, 20

Monnet, Georges, 106

Montargis, 41, 53, 144

Morocco: agriculture in, 20–1, 78–9, 119–20; attempted coups in, 21, 79; military expenditure of, 36; poverty in, 1

Moroccan Royal Air Force, 21n

Morris, William, 138

Mossadeq, Mohammed, 88, 91 & n

Mozambique, 81

Muggeridge, Malcolm, 9

Munich Olympic Games (1972), 14–15, 68

Murora Atoll, 35

Nasser, President G. A., 24

Naxalites, 81

Netherlands: cycle tracks in, 112; pollution in, 28; urbanization of, 60–1, 62, 116; use of manure in, 27; *and see* Holland

New Guinea, 43, 121

*New York Times*, 57

New York, pollution in, 33, 63

New Zealand, 10, 37, 55

Niamey, 77

Spain, 22, 137
Stalin, Joseph, 34; Stalinism, 135, 147, 156
Stockholm conference, 21
*Survivre et Vivre*, 102
Sweden, 140
Switzerland, 14, 27, 64

Taiwan, 38, 125
Tanzania: agriculture in, 25, 78; social system of, 78, 82, 83, 131
Thailand, 92
*Tiers Monde*, 159
Togo, 22
Tokyo: air pollution in, 31, 148; urbanization of, 61
*Torrey Canyon*, 126
Trinidad and Tobago, 74
Truman, President Harry S., 134
Tunisia, 1, 15, 25, 119
Tupamaros, 81

Uganda, 43
United Arab Republic, 23, 24, *and see* Egypt
United Nations, 92, 134; bureacracy of, 94; Committee of Development Planning of, 72–3; founding of, 118, 127; lack of authority of, 103; and New Declaration of the Rights of the Child, 50; 'On Human Survival' conference at, 102; policies of, 13, 27, 71–2, 80, 99, 104
United Nations Conference on Trade and Development (UNCTAD), 69, 135
United Nations Educational, Scientific and Cultural Organization (UNESCO), Edgar Faure Commission of, 138–9, 144
United Nations Children's Fund (UNICEF), 50, 57
United States of America: advertising in, 16, 60, 154; air pollution in, 31–2, 54, 148; arms expenditure of, 16, 36; and arms restrictions, 34, 102; and birth control in Third World, 38; and bombing of Vietnam, 35, 131; control of ocean by, 125; debts of, 71; electricity consumption of, 14; food consumption of, 27; forecasts of, 134; Great Depression in, 65; immigration to, 41; imperialism of, 141, 146; hypocrisy of, 147; motor car density in, 53–4, 55; oil shortage in, 110, 125–6, 128; pollution in, 33, 63; nuclear power of, 14, 34, 35; population growth in, 41, 62; power of, 90; protest movements in, 67, 130; projected effects of nuclear war in, 37; reduction in aid by, 72; reduction in farming land in, 42, 62, 114, 159; and social changes in India, 164; soil erosion in, 21–2; southern plantations of, 75; Soviet imports from, 29; travel expenditure in, 112; urbanization of, 61, 62, 114; use of nitrates in, 28, 29, 122; use of soya bean in, 51; surpluses in, 118; wastage in, 28, 39, 48, 49, 57, 122; water supplies to, 25, 108; wealth in, 10, 49, 130, 154
Upper Volta, 90, 132
Uruguay, 81

Venezuela, 21, 92
Vietnam, North: birth control in, 38, 40, 41; bombing of, 2, 35; metal salvage in, 106; overpopulation of, 43, 62; poverty in, 1; regime of, 4, 131, 155; and US withdrawal, 150; use of fertilizer in, 122; *and see* Vietnam War
Vietnam, South, 1, 125, 146
Vietnam War, 3, 35, 44, 72, 81, 82, 102, 134, 141; casualties of, 55, 131, 157; protests against, 130, 159

179